Collectible Spoons
of the 3rd Reich

with
extensive historical exposition

by

James A. Yannes

Other Books by James A. Yannes

Astonishing Investment Facts and Wisdom
Astonishing Conservative Thoughts, Facts and Humor

Order this book online at www.trafford.com/08-1199
or email orders@trafford.com

Most Trafford titles are also available at major online book retailers.

© Copyright 2009 James A. Yannes.

All rights reserved. No part of this publication may be reproduced, stored in a retrieval system, or transmitted, in any form or by any means, electronic, mechanical, photocopying, recording, or otherwise, without the written prior permission of the author.

Note for Librarians: A cataloguing record for this book is available from Library and Archives Canada at www.collectionscanada.ca/amicus/index-e.html

Printed in Victoria, BC, Canada.

ISBN: 978-1-4251-8695-1

We at Trafford believe that it is the responsibility of us all, as both individuals and corporations, to make choices that are environmentally and socially sound. You, in turn, are supporting this responsible conduct each time you purchase a Trafford book, or make use of our publishing services. To find out how you are helping, please visit www.trafford.com/responsiblepublishing.html

Our mission is to efficiently provide the world's finest, most comprehensive book publishing service, enabling every author to experience success. To find out how to publish your book, your way, and have it available worldwide, visit us online at www.trafford.com/10510

Trafford PUBLISHING

www.trafford.com

North America & international
toll-free: 1 888 232 4444 (USA & Canada)
phone: 250 383 6864 ♦ fax: 250 383 6804
email: info@trafford.com

The United Kingdom & Europe
phone: +44 (0)1865 487 395 ♦ local rate: 0845 230 9601
facsimile: +44 (0)1865 481 507 ♦ email: info.uk@trafford.com

10 9 8 7 6 5 4 3 2

German Law regarding Maker's Marks

In 1884 a law was enacted making .800 the minimum national standard in Germany for silver. In 1886 the use of individual city marks was abolished and replaced by the national mark (reichsmark) of a crescent moon & crown (Halbmond und Krone) representing the entire German state. These marks became compulsory by 1888. The Crescent Moon & Crown are used in conjunction with a decimal silver standard mark, usually .800 or .925 and a maker's mark. Due to the large number of manufacturers and an apparent lack of centralized records, many maker's marks can no longer be identified.

This eagle is a Bruckmann & Sohne maker's mark or Herstellungszeichen

	Pages
Table Of Contents	3 - 6
In Appreciation	6
Introduction,	7 - 15
Special Note & Photo Comment	16
Spoons: Descriptions & Photos,	17 - 177

Personality Spoons

PS-1 Adolf Hitler, Formal Pattern	18 & 19
PS-2 Adolf Hitler, Curved 'AH',	20 & 21
PS-3 Adolf Hitler, Ornamental	22 & 23
PS-4 Adolf Hitler, Raised ribs	24 & 25
PS-5 Eva Braun, Baroque	26 & 27
PS-6 Eva Braun, Parfait Spoon	28 & 29
PS-7 Herman Goering, Arms	30 & 31
PS-8 Herman Goering, RMarshall	32 & 33
PS-9 Heinrich Himmler, Train	34 & 35
PS-10 Heinrich Himmler,	36 & 37
PS-11 Albert Speer,	38 & 39
PS-12 Helmut Weidling	40 & 41
PS-13 Bernard Rust, DH	42 & 43
PS-14 Bernard Rust, DH	44 & 45
PS-15 Dr. Robert Ley, DAF	46 & 47
PS-16 Ernst Kaltenbrunner,	48 & 49
PS-17 Fritz Sauckel	50 & 51
PS-18 Hans Frank	52 & 53

Other Government Spoons

OG-19	NSDAP-Fraktur	54 & 55
OG-20	NSDAP	56 & 57
OG-21	NSDAP / SA Early Version	58 & 59
OG-22	SA Sturmabteilung	60 & 61
OG-23	SA	62 & 63
OG-24	HJ Hitler-Jugend	64 & 65
OG-25	HJ - RFS	66 & 67
OG-26	RAD	68 & 69
OG-27	DR-Deutsche Reichsbahn,	70 & 71
OG-28	DR-AH 205	72 & 73
OG-29	DR-Goering 243	74 & 75
OG-30	Reich Chancellery RK	76 & 77
OG-31	Deutsche Rotes Kreuz	78 & 79
OG-32	RLB, Air Raid Protection	80 & 81
OG-33	Student Federation	82 & 83
OG-34	Eagle, 1942	84 & 85

Wehrmacht - Military Spoons

W-35	Army Mess, W.S.M.42	86 & 87
W-36	Army Mess, "WH"	88 & 89
W-37	Army Mess, 'LGK&F 39	90 & 91
W-38	Army Mess, B.A. F. N. 39	92 & 93
W-39	Army, 1944 commemorative?	94 & 95
W-40	Army H.U.	96 & 97
W-41	Africa Corps D.AK	98 & 99
W-42	Africa Corps D.AK, CA.Krall	100 & 101
W-43	Navy Mess, HHL Rustfrei	102 & 103
W-44	Navy Mess, Blancadur	104 & 105
W-45	Air Force Mess, Droop Tail	106 & 107
W-46	Air Force Mess, Oxydex	108 & 109
W-47	Air Force Officer's Service	110 & 111
W-48	Air Force Officer's Service	112 & 113
W-49	Air Force General Officer's	114 & 115

W-50 Air Force General Officers — 116 & 117

SS Spoons, Introduction — 118 & 119

SS-51 LSSAH, 1st SS Div, V.S.F.	120 & 121
SS-52 LSSAH, Becker	122 & 123
SS-53 LSSAH, "1941", WMF	124 & 125
SS-54 LSSAH, LW	126 & 127
SS-55 2nd SS Div-'Reich', "XX"	128 & 129
SS-56 SS-Reich, LSF	130 & 131
SS-57 SS-Reich, Berndorf	132 & 133
SS-58 SS-Reich, Textured SS	134 & 135
SS-59 3rd SS Div - 'Totenkopf'	136 & 137
SS-60 5th SS Div - 'Wiking'	138 & 139
SS-61 9th SS Div - 'Hohenstaufen'	140 & 141
SS-62 11th SS Div - 'Nordland'	142 & 143
SS-63 Waffen SS	144 & 145
SS-64 SS, Raised SS	146 & 147
SS-65 SS, SS in a double circle,	148 & 149
SS-66 SS - Mocka spoon	150 & 151
SS-67 SS - Wewelsburg, VIP	152 & 153
SS-68 SS - Wewelsburg, RFS	154 & 155
SS-69 SS/Police	156 & 157
SS-70 SS/Police	158 & 159

Miscellaneous

M-71 Adolf Hitler Napkin Ring,	160 & 161
M-72 U-47 Commemorative	162 & 163
M-73 Danziger Werft	164 & 165
M-74 Haus der Deutschen Arbeit	166 & 167
M-75 Officer's Field Service	168 & 169
M-76 Wehrmacht Fieldgear	170 & 171
M-77 Wellner of East German	172 & 173
M-78 Bayerischer Hof Hotel	174 & 175
M-79 Bormann vs Nurnberg	176 & 177

Spoons: Material and length,   178 - 184
Bibliography   185 - 186
Historical Supplement   187 - 198
Addendum   199 - 221
  AD-80 Waffen-SS   200 - 201
  AD-81 Kriegsmarine, no 'M'   202 - 203
  AD-82 NSKOV   204 - 205
  AD-83 HJ-Sportsschule   206 - 207
  AD-84 Heer JRS 41   208 - 209
  AD-85 Deutsche Reichsbahn   210 - 211
  AD-86 SS, Neusilber   212 - 213
  AD-87 K.L. Buchenwald   214 - 215
  AD-88 Deutsche Christen   216 - 217
Things of Interest   218 - 221
Special Note   222
FINI   223

In Appreciation

As an accumulator as opposed to a collector, I am completely reliant on my sources as to the authenticity of the items purchased. As my primary sources, I thank the following people and organizations for their patience, sharing their expertise and delivering excellent spoons..

  Brock's Inc., Decatur, Georgia
  Collector's Guild Inc., Fredericton NB, Canada
  Germania Int'l., Lakemont, GA
  Patton, Terry, Acworth, GA
  Snyder, Charles E.Jr., Bowie, MD

  Thames Army Surplus, Groton, Conn
  Third Reich CA, Sidney, BC Canada
  Third Reich Depot, Conifer, CO
  USMBOOKS, Rapid City, SD
  Witte, David, Little Rock, AR
  WW2GermanMilitaria, Burnaby B. C. Canada

For help on Mystery Maker's Marks:

Paul Raackow of Bestechliste, Berlin, Germany for his kind asistance with the identification of several mystery Makers Marks.

INTRODUCTION

In a recent visit to Munich, we came across a "Third Reich Tour". This was a walking tour which "covers all important facts and sites that played a role in the origin of this black chapter, that ended with the beautiful city of Munich in ruins." With a sub title, "Hitler's Munich." when we asked the tour guide if he was comfortable with the subject matter, he explained that he had been born in the mid 1960's and that for him, the Second World War was history. He said his grand parents and his parents wanted nothing to do with memories of the war. We even have a friend who was born in the 1930's and baptized 'Adolf' who had his name changed out of revulsion for what had occurred. This encounter brought to mind the changed opinion of Napoleon who had caused the deaths of millions and was condemned by the world in the mid 19th century only to now be a hero of France. This is not to say the Hitler and the 3rd Reich will ever be revered like Napoleon but that as time passes, perceptions dim and places and items take on a historical patina.

There are a number of very interesting Third Reich locations available to anyone with an interest in the historical aspects of what will undoubtedly be the defining military effort in history. My wife and I have visited all the sites to be mentioned but unfortunately when we made our visits, I had no intention of writing about them so the descriptions will be from memory and with little detail.

Munich: This is a good place to start as Hitler called Munich the "Capital of the Movement". There are two walking tours, the two and one half hour "Third Reich Tour" and a 5 hour "Extended Third Reich Tour". I highly recommend a down town hotel so you can walk to the start point in the Marienplatz. Much of the "Nazi" architecture has survived such as the The Fuhrerbau" which is a music school and open to the public - the place where Chamberlin received his 'Peace in our time' paper from Hitler. and the mirror image, Administration building. A one day side trip to Bad Wiessee to visit the site of Hitler's arrest of SA leader Ernst Rohm as depicted in a History Channel episode. The hotel has been renamed 'Hotel Lederer am See' on Tegernseer Tal. The staff is not interested in discussing the matter but there is a very pleasant bar overlooking the lake for cake and coffee.

Dresden: The Munchner Platz Memorial This was a central execution site where some 1,300 were beheaded by guillotine. A short drive away is Pirna's Sonnenstein Memorial at Struppener Strasse 22 where some 13,720 mentally ill and retarded patients were gassed - legally - under "Action T4".

Wunsdorf: This area south of Berlin has historically been the headquarters for the Army Command. The concept was to keep the military out of Berlin proper so as to isolate the political center from the military center. Here was the Zeppelin communications bunker the teletype and telephone exchange for the army command and Wehrmacht transportation corps. Also the Maybach Bunker complex for Army command staff and the "Winkel" air raid shelters. Tours here are 1.5 hours or special tours of 5 hours. The tour center is at Gutenbergstrasse 1. Note: As per W.W.II agreements, the Maybach bunker complex was blown up by the Russians but they kept the Zeppelin bunker for its communications as well as it was felt to be atomic bomb survivable.

Wewelsburg: This triangular castle (one of only 3 in the world) was the ritual headquarters of the SS. It has an extensive museum, well worth the trip.

Quedlinburg: The cathedral was taken over by the SS and in 1937, the bones of King Heinrich I (875-936) were interred. Heinrich Himmler reportedly believed he was the reincarnation of King Heinrich. Himmler visited the tomb periodically and communed with the King who had defeated the Slavs.

So much for travel suggestions.

My first disclaimer: I am not an expert on 3rd Reich tableware! In fact, I am not really a collector. I am an accumulator. My interests change with time and several years ago I bought a Hitler spoon and used it for several years in my morning coffee. Then I saw an Eva Braun spoon and it seemed appropriate to join them together. This led to picking up various spoons over the years. As it is obvious, my collection is a type collection, with emphasis on breadth rather than depth. As a rank amateur, I have relied on my sources to deliver correct material. So I challenge the reader to point out the inevitable fakes. The intent of the book is to broaden the coverage of this interesting area. Why spoons? Primarily due to being unable to find knife or fork display cases. I could only find spoon display cases and a spoon is a very useable utensil in its own right. Unlike a knife, I have seen no cases where someone has committed suicide by slashing their wrists with a spoon, with a possible exception of the California penal system, and unlike a fork, I have never read newspaper reports of emergency room removals of a spoon from from someone's neck. To summarize, spoons are friendly, non threatening utensils and easily displayed. They also entice their clandestine collection. Thomas Breyette, the author of the definitive book on German Tank Destruction Badges told me the story of one of the recipients of the TDB purloining one of Adolf Hitler's spoons as he retired from his award luncheon hosted by the Fuhrer.

Regarding "Hitler's" personal flatware variations: The only reference books I have are, <u>Treasure Trove - The Looting of the Third Reich</u> by Charles E. Snyder, Jr. Major USAF (Retired) and <u>"Liberated" Adolf Hitler Memorabilia</u> by Mark D. Griffith, M.D. In the Griffith book on page 15 he illustrates and states "close-up of the handles illustrating five of the six different patterns of silverware." where as Snyder illustrates 16 different patterns on pages 37 to 41. As always, these types of inquiries will remain somewhat of a mystery as the records no longer exist. As an example, I purchased a Kriegsmarine binocular, maker marked 'beh' for the manufactured Leitz. After the war Leitz became Leica who in turn destroyed all W.W.II. Leitz records. Even inquiries to the U.S. Government and Corning Glass proved unsuccessful so that determining the production history is apparently lost forever. You may ask, why Corning - After the war, the U.S. Government sent teams to Germany to retrieve all technical advancements that Germany had made during the war and to bring all the technology back to the U.S. for evaluation and to make use of anything of value. Corning got the optics advancements. This was likened to looting grandma's attic. You may recall that during the Carter administration, tons of W.W.II German material related to the manufacture of petroleum products from coal were pored over in an effort to find some economic solution to the "energy crises' of that period.

The Spoons are organized into sections.

Section I

Section I includes items associated with specific personalities. In some cases the spoons carry the initials of the owner and in others, a pattern strictly associated with a specific person. The easy examples are the Adolf Hitler spoons marked with his personal eagle straddled with his initials "A" and "H". An example of the second variation would be a Hans Frank spoon which carries the/ his official state pattern of the Governor General of Poland. These pieces are usually listed by the associated owners name.

Included are representational pieces from:

    Adolf Hitler
    Eva Braun
    Herman Goering
    Heinrich Himmler
    Albert Speer
    Helmut Weidling
    Bernard Rust
    Dr. Robert Ley
    Ernst Kaltenbrunner
    Fritz Sauckel
    Hans Frank

Section II

Section II includes "Other Government". Under the 3rd Reich, essentially all organizations were either in the government or were eliminated, the labor unions being a prime example.

Included are representational pieces from:

N.S.D.A.P. - Nationalsozialistische Deutsche Arbeiterpartei, (National Socialist German Worker's Party)
SA - Sturmabtellung - Storm troopers
HJ - Hitler Youth
RAD - Reichs Arbeitsdienst - National Labor Service, dated 1936
DR - Deutsche Reichsbahn - German National Railways
RK - Neureichkanzlei - New National Chancellery, Berlin
DRK - Deutsches Rotes Kreuz - German Red Cross
RLB - Reichs Luftschutzbund - National Air Raid Protection League
NSDStB - National Socialistische Studenten Bund - National Socialist Student Association

Section III

Section III includes representative spoons from the Wehrmacht - Armed Services:

    Heer - Army
    Heer / D.AK - Deutsches Africa Korps - Africa Corps
    KM - Kriegsmarine - Navy
    Luftwaffe - Air Force

Section IV

Section IV includes SS spoons:

    1st SS Panzer Division - LSSAH
    2nd SS Panzer Division - Reich
    3rd SS Panzer Division - Totenkopf

5th SS Panzer Division - Wiking
9th SS Panzer Division - Hohenstaufen
11th SS Panzer Division - Nordland
Waffen SS
SS only, variations
SS Wewelsburg
SS / Police

Section V

Section V includes miscellaneous items:

An Adolf Hitler Napkin Ring
U-47 commemorative spoon
Union spoon from early 1933
Army Officer's Field Besteck
Army Field Gear Folding Spoon & Fork
Wellner of East Germany
Bayerischer Hof Hotel
Bormann vs Nurnberg ?

Common Markings and general comments:

Rustfrei = Rust Free (Stainless Steel)
Nicht Rostend = None Rusting
Gusstahl Solingen = Cast Steel
Mess Hall (Kantine) & Galley (Schiffskuche):
Teaspoon (Teeloffel), Tablespoon (Esloffel)
Serving Ladle (Schopfloffel)
Fork (Gabel), Desert Fork (Sussgabel)
Knife (Messer)
Table knife (Tischmesser) - two piece construction with nickel/ silver plated stainless steel blade and silver handle.
RZM = Reichzeugmeisterei (National Equipment Quartermaster) founded in 1934 by the NSDAP as

a Reich Hauptamt (State Central Office) The RZM procured and distributed items, approved designs, insured quality, supervised standardization and compliance to specifications.

RB = (Reichsbetrieb nummer) RB numbers replaced Manufacturer's names on products in 1942 to conceal the manufacturers name and therefore location from allied bombing.

Heer

W.H. = Wehrmacht Heeres (Armed Forces Army) Army field, folding cutlery sets (Essbesteck) of either Knife/Spoon/Fork or Spoon/ Fork combinations are typically of aluminum for weight considerations

Kriegsmarine

An "M" indicates Kriegsmarine and can appear either above or below the eagle

The eagles can vary with simple 3 lined wings to 5 full feathered wings as on C&CW produced items.

Luftwaffe

Fl.U.V. = Flieger Unterkunft Verwaltung = Flight Barracks Administration

Eagles come in two variations: Early version with "Drooped Tail" on items marked up through 1941 Later version with "Straight Tail" on items dated 1942 and later

SS

SS-WVHA = SS-Wirtschafts und Verwaltungs Hauptamt (SS-Economic and Administration Department) - responsible for issuing personal equipment items

SS-T.V. = SS-Totenkopfvberbande
SS-Death's Head Units)
SS-W.B. = SS-Wachverbande (SS-Guard Units)
RZM/SS = SS items Quality controlled by RZM
1934 to 1943

The post Nazi German Government's directions regarding 3rd Reich material: Relevant sections of German Law - summary of section § 86, 86a:
"Items that are used for making propaganda for a party or group which is classed as unconstitutional or forbidden, even if they act outside Germany, may not be spread inside Germany. This applies for items made to propagate ideas that correspond with the ideas of the "Third Reich". They might not be made, kept, imported or exported. The punishment may be prison (up to three years) or a fine.

This does not apply if those items are used in order to inform others, repel actions that are aimed against the constitution, if they are used in art, science, research, teaching, or to report about historical events or similar purposes.

If you use or show symbols or signs used by parties or groups that can be classified as unconstitutional, or if you manufacture, keep, export or import those, you may be punished (three years imprisonment or fine). You may not use or spread items that display or contain those signs or symbols, e.g. flags, insignia, uniforms (or parts of uniforms), mottos and forms of greeting. You may also not use or spread signs or symbols that look similar to those. This does not apply if those items are used in order to inform others, repel actions that are aimed against the constitution, if they are used in art, science, research, teaching, or to report about historical events or similar purposes."

Special note

Albert Kesselring, Luftwaffe Field Marshal summed up the philosophical differences between the 3rd Reich's Military services as : "the 'republican' Army, the 'imperialist' Navy and the 'national socialist' Luftwaffe. These adjectives reveal the patent disunity of the Service's attitudes."

These disparate attitudes can be seen in their spoons via the presentation of the Nazi swastika to the traditional national eagle via the Army's middle of the road, the Navy's minimal and the Luftwaffe's excessive presentation of the swastika..

Photo Comment

Having made contact with several photographers as well as advertising at photography schools for assistance in the photography of the spoons - - all of which ended unsuccessful when informed of the number of photos required. As a result, I purchased a Canon A630, 8.0 Mega Pixel digital camera, tripods, lights, photo boxes etc., signed up for Apple's onetoone consulting and after taking hundreds of photos, have decided to go with these. At times i have used 'artistic license' by taking oblique photos where it was not possible to get a good straight on photo due to reflections etc. This sometimes makes the spoons appear to be none symmetrical. I can assure you that German spoons are symmetrical. All photos were first edited with Apple's iPhoto '08 and then transferred to Apple's iWork's - Pages for final placement and adjustment. I still show up in one of the spoon bowels. Special thanks to Apple's Elizabeth for her patience and guidance, above and beyond the call of duty. On the other hand, Apple's 'Pages' was a constant disappointment!

THE SPOONS

"If he does really think that there is no distinction between virtue and vice, why, sir when he leaves our houses, let us count our spoons." - Samuel Johnson

"The louder he talked of his honour, the faster we counted our spoons." - Ralph Waldo Emerson

18

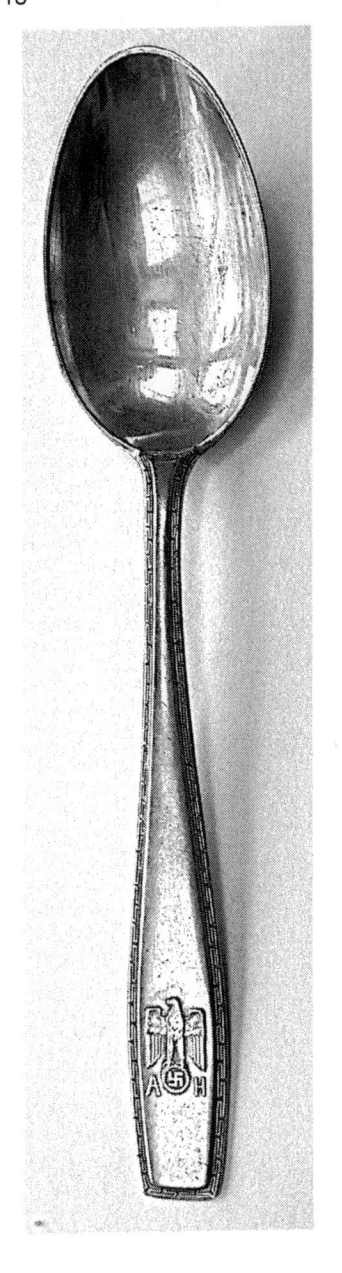

PS-1
L = 146 mm / 5 3/4"

PERSONALITY SPOONS

PS-1 Hitler, Adolf "Formal Pattern"
(1889 - 1945)

Tea spoon - Teeloffel: This is the most recognizable and available, likewise the most sought after of the Hitler memorabilia. As per Billy Price's, Hitler, the Unknown Artist "it is well known that the Fuhrer had personally designed these formal pieces featuring the "Fuhrer Adler" (the Leaders Eagle) with "A" and "H" to either side of the wreathed, static swastika in its talons." Much of Hitler's silver flatware was manufactured by the firm of P. Bruckmann & Sohne of Heilbronn an ancient town on the Neckar River in Wurttemberg. Bruckmann, (1805 - 1973), was one of the leading silver manufacturers in Germany. As a gift for Hitler's 50th birthday on 20 April 1939, Bruckmann presented some 3,000 pieces made up of six complete sets of 500 pieces, one set each for his 'Berghof' (Mountain Home), the guest house at Obersalzberg and the "Adlerhorst" (the Eagles Nest) nearby; the Nazi Party's "Braune Haus" (Brown House) in Munich; the Prinzregertenplatz apartment in Munich and the "Reichschancellery" Chancellery in Berlin. The tableware, needing to be harder and more durable, were made of .800 silver while the matching service pieces were made of .925 silver. The state formal pattern has a Greek Key "Meander" pattern, (representing the Greek river Meander as Hitler was an admirer of ancient Greece). Design assistance is sometimes attributed to Frau Professor and Architect Gerdy Troost (wife of Hitler's foremost architect - Paul Ludwig Troost) in any case, Hitler oversaw the effort.

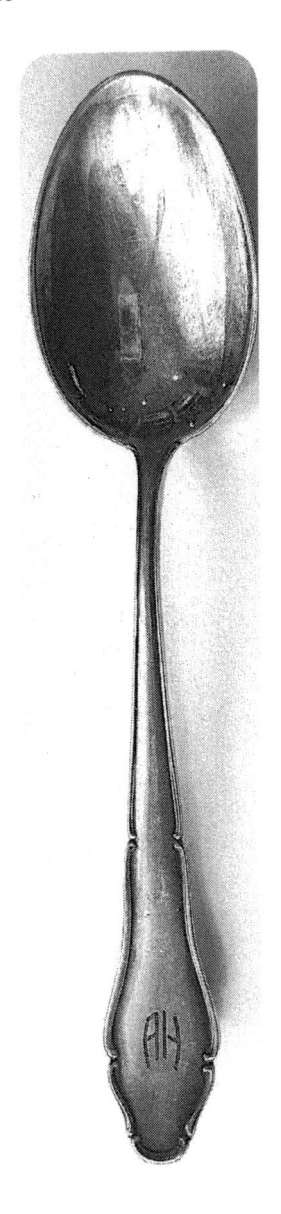

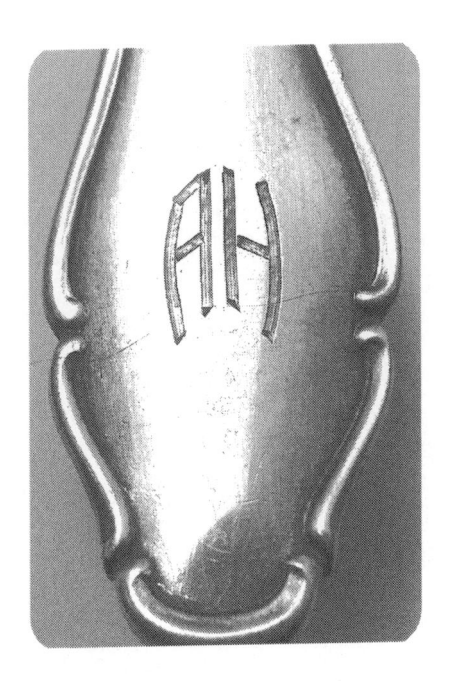

PS-2
L = 148 mm / 5 13/16"

PS-2 **Hitler's**, Curved AH monogram

Teaspoon. With 'Reichsmark'* 800 and the maker's mark of Lutz & Weiss of Pforzheim, founded 1882. (a stylized L over W inside a shield)

The curved monogram was also used on his crystal ware in the Obersalzberg area. Distinctive and unique to the Berghof, Hitler's mountain retreat in the Alps per Mark D. Griffith's Liberated - Adolf Hitler Memorabilia, published 1985, page 14. "The "AH" is side by side with outer edges curved convex (outward). The top centers of the letters form a peak in the middle and the bottoms of the letters are proportionally indented. This spoon has the "flattop A" and is executed in 4 strokes, one for the convex outer side, one for the interior vertical, one for the top of the A and one for the middle. The H is virtually a mirror image of the "A" without the top stroke and is executed in three strokes."

Hitler Trivia: His uniforms are divided into 3 periods / styles:
1. Kampfzeit: The brown shirt with Sam Brown cross belt 1920's - 1933
2. Statesman: Fine brown tunic with white shirt 1933 - 1939
3. Victory or Death: Field Gray tunic with white shirt 1939 - 1945 (with SS sleeve eagle)

.

(Kampfzeit = Period of struggle)

22

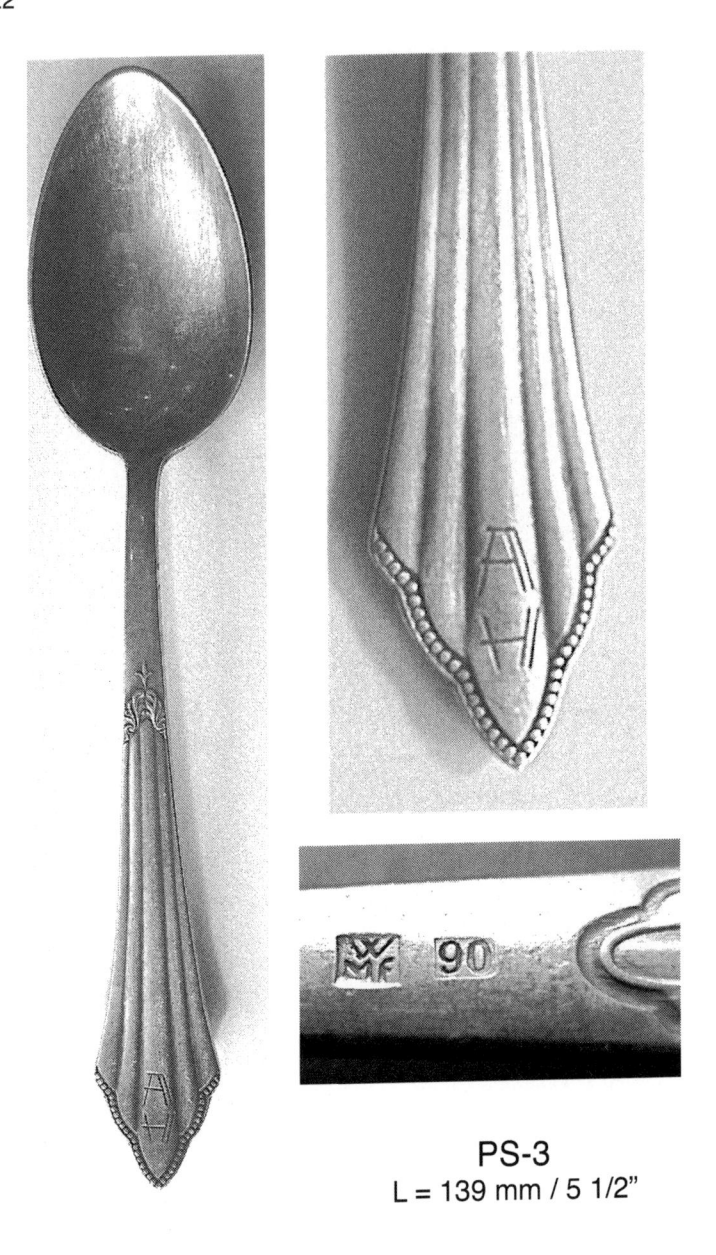

PS-3
L = 139 mm / 5 1/2"

PS-3   **Hitler**, Ornamented

Teaspoon. From 1/2 of length in five waves, terminated with 41 dots patterned on obverse and reverse. Hallmark: W over MF (Wurttembergische Metallwarenfabrik, Geislingen 1853 to the present) 90   Monogram: A over H, struck.

Note: Hitler's complimentary silver service pieces and heavier items such as coffee & tea services, trays, coasters, gravy boats, etc. typically came from August Wellner & Sohne, of Aue (1854 -) Germany's other leading silver manufacturer.

Hitler trivia: His favorite part of the meal was desert. He relished cakes and pies, and ice cream with strawberries drowned in mounds of whipped cream. He drowned his coffee and tea with sugar and cream. He favored Fachingen Heilwasser mineral water.

24

PS-4
L = 134 mm / 5 1/4"

PS-4 **Hitler,** Alpaca*

Teaspoon. Triple raised ribs on front, 3 pair of matched ribbons. Hallmark: Wellner with an elephant over 'alpaca'*. Block A over H.

Fact: Hitler's income; By 1944, some 12.5 million copies of Mein Kampf had been printed with royalties to Hitler. He also collected royalties on the use of his likeness on postage stamps making him a millionaire. His NAZI party membership number was 7.

*Alpaca / Alpacca Silver - Also known in english as 'German Silver' or Nickel Silver and in french as maillechort is an alloy composed of nickel, copper and zinc - contains NO silver. This metal was developed by the Wellner Company of Aue in Saxony. (Typical Alpaca formulation: Copper 65%, Zinc 23% and Nickel 12%.) The elephant was a Wellner trademark.

Trivia: The SS used Alpaca at many of its facilities and this service may have been a gift from the SS or used at SS functions.

26

PS-5
L = 142 mm / 5 10/16"

PS-5 **Braun,** Eva
(1912-1945)

Teaspoon. Pattern: Baroque, high relief asymmetrical. Hallmark: 46 Jurst 50. Monogram: EB Butterfly engraved. The EB Butterfly logo was designed by Albert Speer, perhaps her best friend and closest confidant at Obersalzberg.

In the 16 years of the Braun-Hitler relationship, Eva, spent the last ten years of her life virtually sequestered in the Berghof where Hitler provided everything for her. He even assigned her the monetary rights to some of his photos, taken by Hoffmann, which made her financially independent.

> Two of her surviving quotes from 1945 - "I want to be a beautiful corpse" and after the wedding, "You may safely call me Frau Hitler."
>
> She practiced Yoga

28

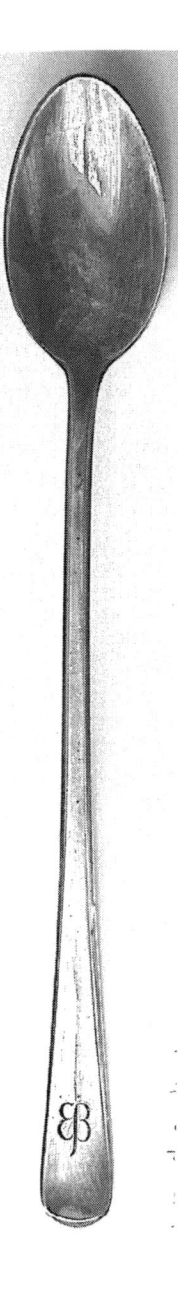

PS-6
L = 212 mm / 8 3/8"

PS-6 **Braun**, Eva

Ice Tea Spoon, Long Handled, **"EB"** butterfly monogram, Very Plain symmetrical design with the single line engraved. Maker marked: 'EKA' block initial, 90 - 1 1/4 on the reverse.

> Per Albert Speer, " Eva Braun especially delighted in showing off her new patterns at any opportunity, frequently using a different pattern at each place of the table and asking her guests which patterns they preferred."
>
> Braun Trivia: She was 23 years Hitler's junior and first met him when she was 17 in 1929.

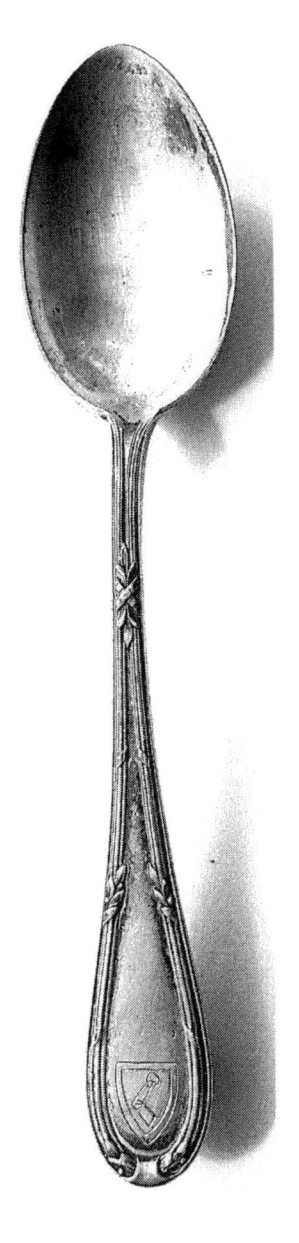

PS-7
L = 137 mm / 5 7/8"

PS-7 **Goering, Hermann**
(1893-1946)

Teaspoon. The Goering Coat of Arms, a right arm raised, facing right, grasping a ring. Pattern: Triple raised ribs, both sides, front and rear wheat pattern. Hallmark: 800; RM; torch. Monogram: Goring coat of arms in unribbed variant.

Goering had literally dozens of sets of silver and thousands of individual pieces of Besteck (cutlery). He was given sets from France, England and numerous German districts. The Reichsmarschal did not favor Hitler's Wellner or Bruckmann but was partial to others such as Hulse. Goering was the chief procurement officer of the military, the leader of the four-year plan, and for all intents and purposes - a Head of State.

On Goering's 45th birthday - 12 Jan 1938, He accepted an exquisite Serves centerpiece from all the workers in his Four-Year Plan, who, at Goerings behest, and most cheerfully he was sure, had received their last month's salaries deducted of 5% for the purchase of the gift.

>Goering Trivia: He famously stated that, "I intend to plunder, and to do it thoroughly."

PS-8
L = 145 mm / 5 11/16"

PS-8 **Goering**

Teaspoon. His Reichsmarshall Coat of Arms, Pattern: recessed rib, both sides, full length of handle. Hallmark: unknown RM 800. Monogram: Type 3 Reichsmarschall Eagle

> Goring Trivia - <u>As Reichminister of the Hunt</u> he outlawed: Horse-and-hound hunting, Shooting from cars, Claw and wire traps, Artificial lights to attract quarry and the issuance of hunting licenses to poor marksman.

PS-9
L = 141 mm / 5 1/2"

PS-9 **Himmler, Heinrich**
(1900 - 1945)

Teaspoon. **Himmer's Train Pattern,** Runic **HH** Monogram Smooth art deco with raised rib, full length of handle. Hallmark: B (Bruckmann), a locomotive engine and (a content mark) 90 indicating heavy silver plate. Monogram: HH in block letters.

Reichsfuhrer-SS, Head of the Gestapo and the Waffen-SS and later Minister of Interior from 1943 to 1945. After Hitler, the most powerful man in Nazi Germany during 1944 & 1945.

As a leading Nazis vegetarian, Himmler launched programs to stop the SS from eating artificial honey, was against food companies using refined flower and white sugar and banned cigarettes in the Allgemeine-SS based on Nazi medical research in the early 1930's linking both cigarettes and asbestos to lung cancer.

Trivia: Himmler's private train was first named Heinrich later changed to Steiermark and in 1944, temporarily named Transport 44.

36

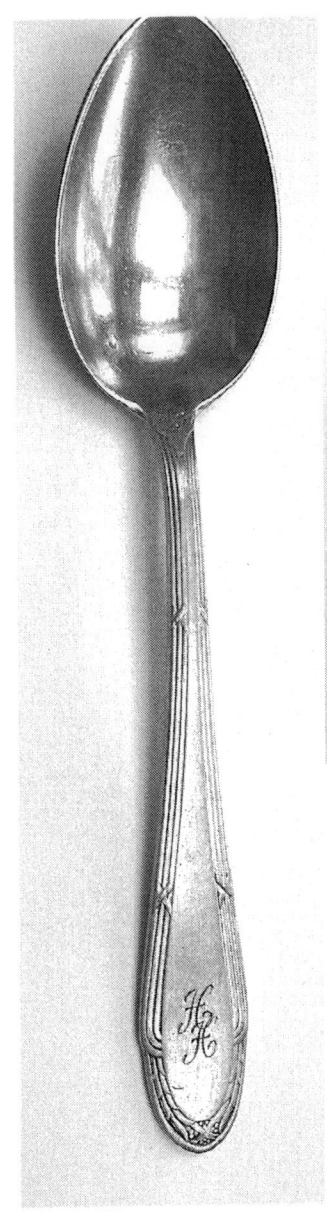

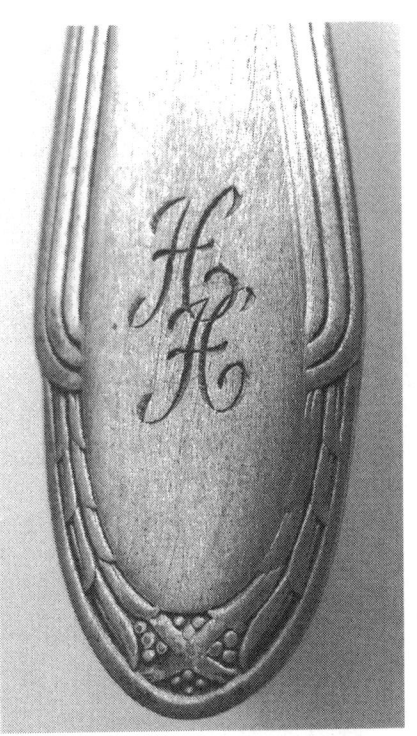

PS-10
L = 138 mm / 5 7/16"

PS-10 **Himmler,**

Teaspoon. **HH** script Monogram. Triple raised ribs on front only, Raised plain rib on back. Hallmark: Ostrich (emu?) in diamond cartouche and block 'WMF 18' (Wurttembergische Metallwarenfabrik, Geislingen founded in 1853 and still in operation). Monogram: Hand engraved script, partially intertwined vertical HH

Trivia - This failed chicken farmer actually received a diploma in agricultural chemistry from Munich Technical in 1922. He favored a green pencil for signing orders and documents, green ink being a prerogative of government ministers His Nazi party number: 14,303. He joined the SS in 1925 with a membership number of 168. He held Blood Order #3.

During the 1930's, he is quoted. "I'm Party member number 2."

PS-11
L = 140 mm / 5 1/2"

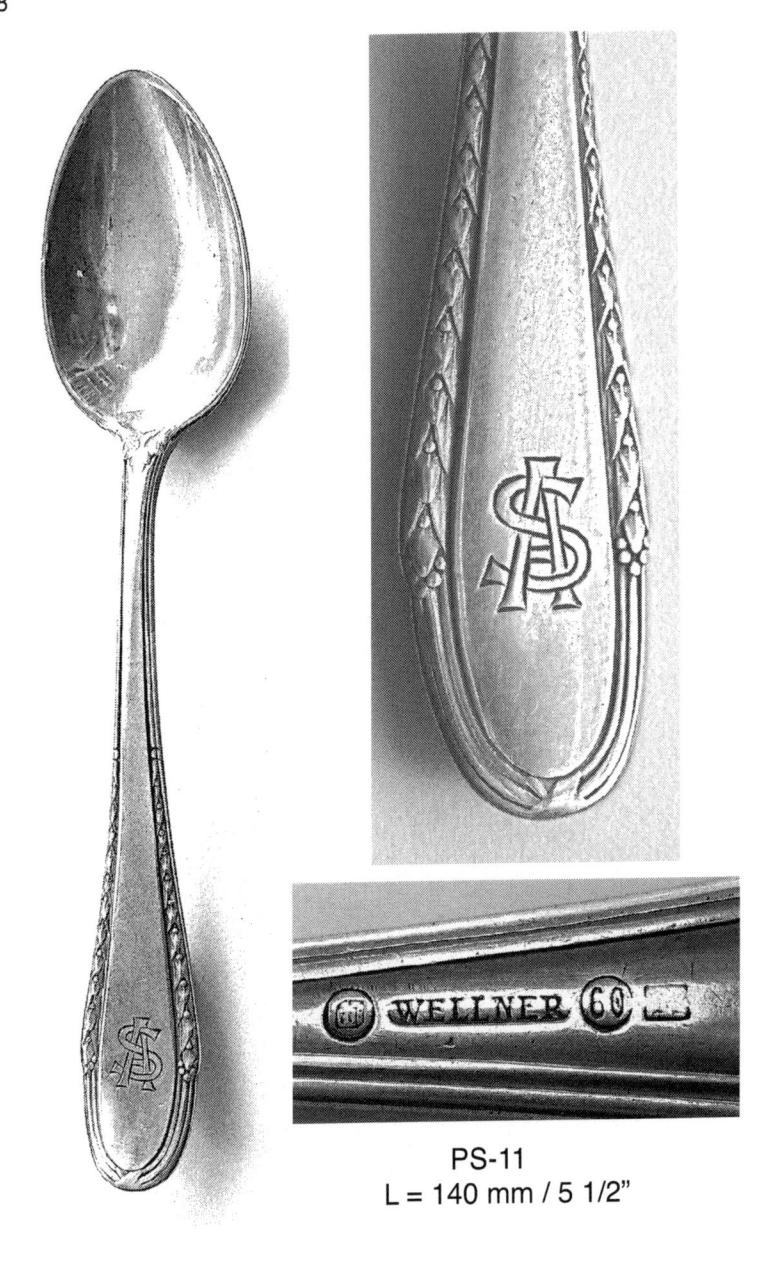

PS-11 Speer, Albert
(1905 - 1981)

Teaspoon. '**AS**': Hallmark: Wellner 60. He personally designed the monogram of Intertwined, block AS

As Hitler's architect he designed and supervised the construction of both the new Reich Chancellery in Berlin (arguably the most profound statement of 'NAZI" architecture and referred to as the most beautiful building ever constructed) and the Party palace in Nuremberg. Reich Minister for Armaments and War Production from February 1942 to 1945. On 1 November 1944, Speer instituted the Notprogramm (emergency program) virtually halting all aircraft manufacture except that of jets and single engine fighters. He reorganized war production and in spite of massive allied bombing attacks raised the 1941 production of front-line machines of 9,540 and heavy tanks of 2,900 to 35,350 front-line machines and 17,300 tanks, as well as raising overall fighter aircraft production to 3,000 a month in 1944 with FW-190's reaching 1,000 per month with some 20,000+ having been produced. Over 30,000 ME-109's were produced. Speer's efforts probably prolonging the war by at least 2 years. His NAZI party number was 474,481

40

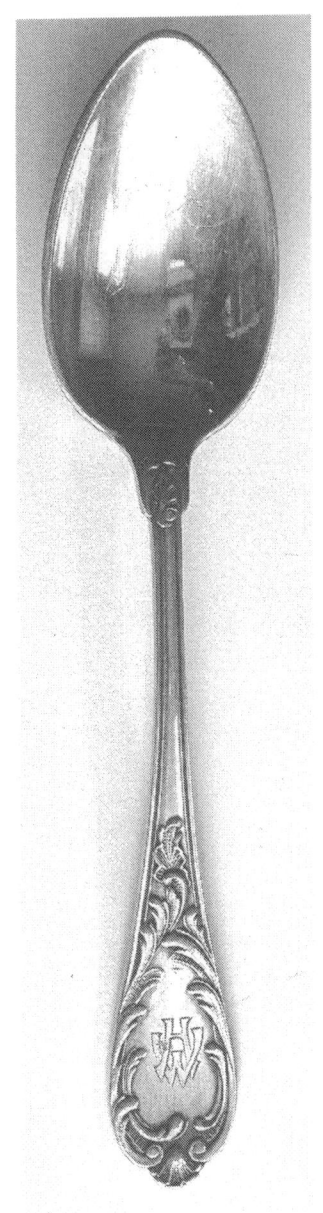

PS-12
L = 143 MM / 5 5/8"

PS-12 Weiding, Helmut (1891 - 1955)
(General of the Artillery - 2nd highest regular Army rank)

Teaspoon. His personal pattern of **'HW'** on the obverse.. Maker marked on the reverse: 'die - 4 & 2 showing, '"Wellner" and content marked '90' and '21' pennyweight silver.

In 1944 he was awarded the Knights Cross with Oak Leaves and Swords. In 1945, he was appointed defense commandant of Berlin and the General in Command of the LXI Panzer Group. The Soviet forces under Marshall Zukhov had 2,500,000 troops, 6,000 tanks and 40,000 artillery pieces facing 300,000 men, many of them Hitler Youth down to the age of 12! The Soviets lost 400,000+ vs 300,000 German civilian and military casualties. He surrendered Berlin on 2 May 1945, was captured by the Soviets, condemned to 25 years in prison and died in Russian captivity in 1955. The **HW** monogram on the obverse has letters intertwined outlined block style.

During the April 1945 defense of Berlin, he is quoted regarding the use of Hitler Youth, "You cannot sacrifice these children for a cause that is already lost."

PS-13 T
L = 210 mm / 8 1/4"

PS-13 **Rust, Bernard's**
(1883-1945)

Tablespoon & Demitasse spoon. **'DH'** for Deutsche-Hochschule, short-form for German Higher Education. - This is his Ministry's official state pattern. Table spoon with "DH" below the national eagle on the reverse side of the spoon. Maker Marked: BR(acia). HENNEBERG BM, a scale in a circle followed by '90' in a square.

Prior to WWI, he was a senior master at a secondary school. WWI: Lieutenant, suffered a serious head wound - Iron Cross 1st class. During April 1934, appointed Reich Minister of Science, Education and Popular Culture till 1945. Purged all Jews from the universities. Dismissed over 1,000 professors including a number of Nobel Prize winners thus hindering German science studies. Rust reported that he had "liquidated the school as an institution of intellectual acrobatics." Committed suicide on 8 May 1945 by gunshot.

PS-14 D
L = 109 mm / 4 5/16"

PS-14 **Rust, Bernard**

Small silver demitasse spoon marked "**DH**" below the national eagle on the obverse. DH for "Deutsche-Hochschule" or German Higher Education, his official state pattern. Maker Marked on the reverse: 'Br Henneberg BM' a scale in a circle, and '90' in a square.

Among the Nobel prize winners he had dismissed: Albert Einstein, James Franck, Fritz Haber, Otto Warburg and Otto Meyerhof. His comment, "We must have a new Aryan generation at the universities, or else we will lose the future."

Note: One dealer ascribed the 'DH' mark to the Deutscher Hof Hotel although most hotels mark their full name on their cutlery.

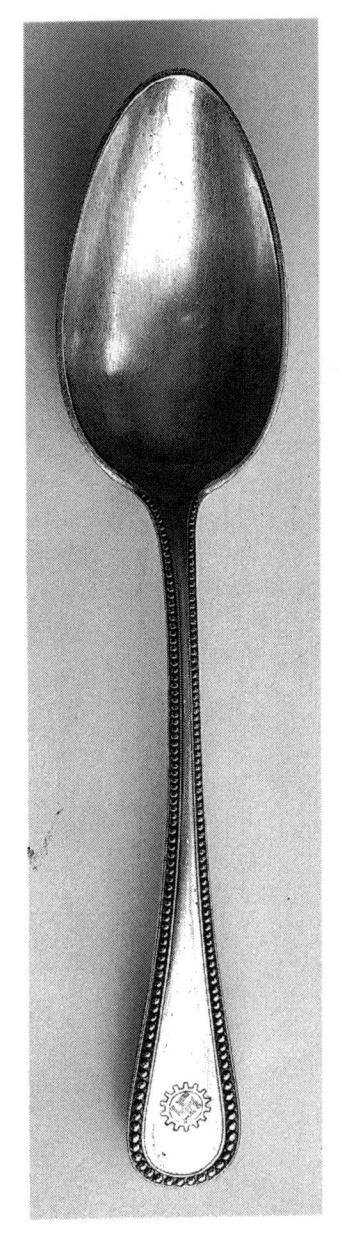

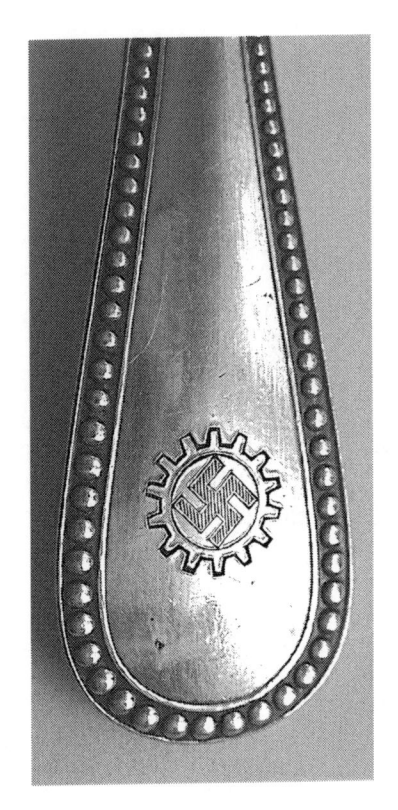

PS-15
L = 216 mm / 8 1/2"

PS-15 Ley, Dr. Robert
(1890-1945)

Tablespoon. **'DAF'** for Deutsche Arbeitsfront - German Labour Front; Tablespoon owned by DAF leader Dr. Robert Ley and carries his Ministry's official state pattern on the obverse. Other patterns: Beaded ribs. both sides, front and back, the length of the handle. Maker marked: a Die in a circle, "WELLNER", "90" in a circle, "45" in a square. By far, much more rare than Hitler's flatware pieces.

DAF with 25 Million members was composed of all trade unions, corporate and professional associations and might better be translated as "Work Force" since the organization included both employers and employees. He also headed the Kraft Durch Freude - 'Strength through Joy' & the Volkswagen factory (no VW's were ever delivered). The DAF emblem was a cogged wheel (Zahnrad) with 14 teeth encompassing a mobile swastika. Dr. Ley committed suicide on 24 October 1945.

Commenting on the trade unions, "Ideologically speaking, the class war was anchored in the trade unions. and the trade unions lived off this."

His nickname: "Reich Drunk Master."

48

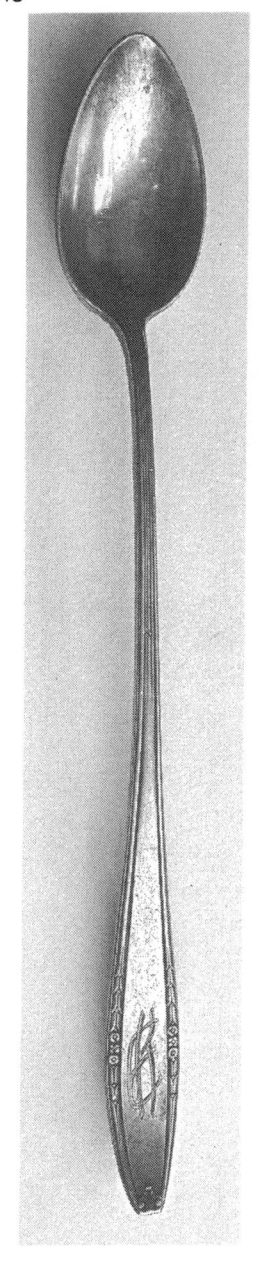

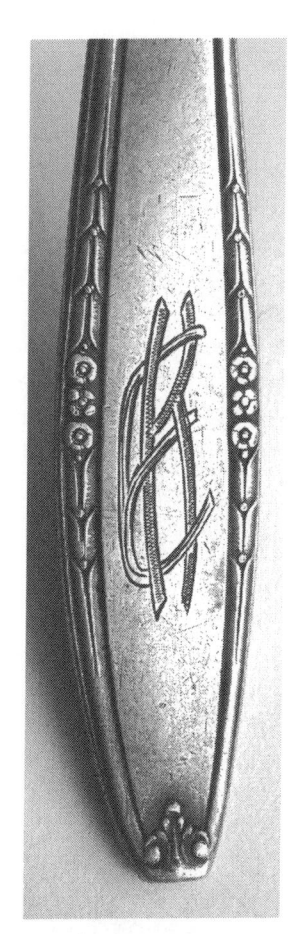

PS-16
L = 224 mm / 8 13/16"

PS-16 Kaltenbrunner, Dr. Ernst
(1903-1946)

Ice tea / parfait spoon. **'EK'** His personal pattern. Maker marked: 'AWS' in a square box (August Wellner & Sohne), an elephant, '100' in a circle and '24' in a square box. The AWS maker mark was used by Wellner from 1928 to 1938. The EK on the obverse is double lined with highlights between. Front and back symmetrical with 3 flowers straddling the initials.

A lawyer and fanatical Austrian Nazi. He along with Seyes-Inquart were the leaders of the Austrian SS from 1934, prior to Anschluss in 1938. In January 1943 he became the 2nd and last Chief of the Reich Main Security Office, (RSHA) succeeding Heydrich with a rank of SS-Obergruppenfuhrer.. Under his tireless direction, the RSHA was responsible for hunting down and exterminating several million civilians, primarily Jews in the East. Hanged in Nuremberg on 16 October 1946.

Nicknamed "The Callous Ox". NAZI party number 300,179

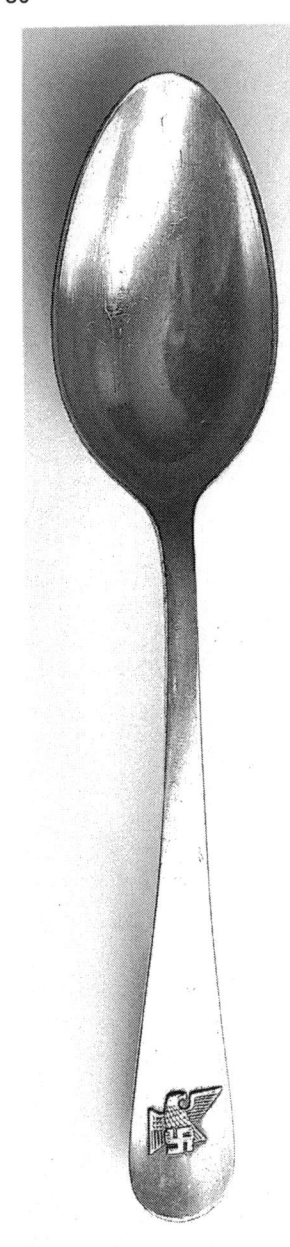

PS-17
L = 213 mm / 8 7/16"

PS-17 **Sauckel, Fritz**
(1984-1946)

Tablespoon, marked on the obverse with his State pattern 'Thuringian Eagle', with its broken wing. Maker marked: "Bruckmann 90" on the reverse.

As the General Plenipotentiary for the Distribution of Labour (Generalbevollmächtigter für den Arbeitseinsatz), 1942 - 1945 he was responsible for directing the deportation of some 5 million slave laborers from the occupied territories, primarily Poland, Ukraine and other eastern countries, to work in German war related industries. He rose from Thuringia's district manager in 1925 to Governor in 1933. He was also both an honorary SA and SS General. At Nuremberg he was "shocked in his innermost soul" to find out about the Nazi atrocities. His most remembered defense, "just following orders".

> Trivia: Sauckel's workers quotas were set by Albert Speer. Speer's labor shortage was primarily due to the prohibition on using German women in industrial jobs. During the Nuremberg trial in 1946 Sauckel pointed at Albert Speer and said, "There is a man you should hang." Speer was sentenced to 20 years. Sauckel was hanged on 16 Oct 1946.

52

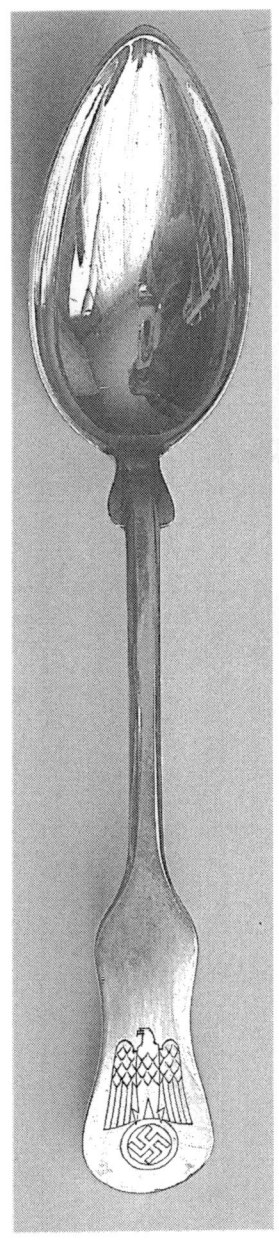

PS-18
L = 217 mm / 8 9/16"

PS-18 **Frank, Dr. Hans**
(1900 - 1946)

Tablespoon, The obverse carries his machine incised, official state pattern of the Governor General of Poland. Maker marked on the reverse with: '45' in a square, '90' in a circle, "ART. KRUPP", their trademark 'Bear with 'ART KRUPP' over and "BERNDORF" under" followed by 'BERNDORF'.

With an IQ of 130, the Nazi Party's leading jurist and Governor General of Poland. Prior to 1933, as Hitler's lawyer he successfully defended Hitler in several hundred actions and afterwards become Reich Minister of Justice. Out of favor with Hitler, he was sent to Poland in 1939 as punishment where he earned the unofficial title of 'slayer of Poles'. Hitler's direction to Frank, "The task which I give you is a devilish one...Other people to who territories are entrusted would ask, 'What will you construct?' I shall ask the opposite." In October 1939 Frank said, "The Poles shall be the slaves of the German Reich." and in 1944, "I have not hesitated to declare that when a German is shot, up to 100 Poles shall be shot too." Hanged as a war criminal in Nuremberg 16 Oct 1946.

Note: Identical tableware has been represented (by the same dealer as on page 45) as from the 'Castle Klessheim' located near Salzburg, Austria, a luxurious government guest residence maintained to house dignitaries waiting to see Hitler at the Burghof. This was vigorously denied by my source.

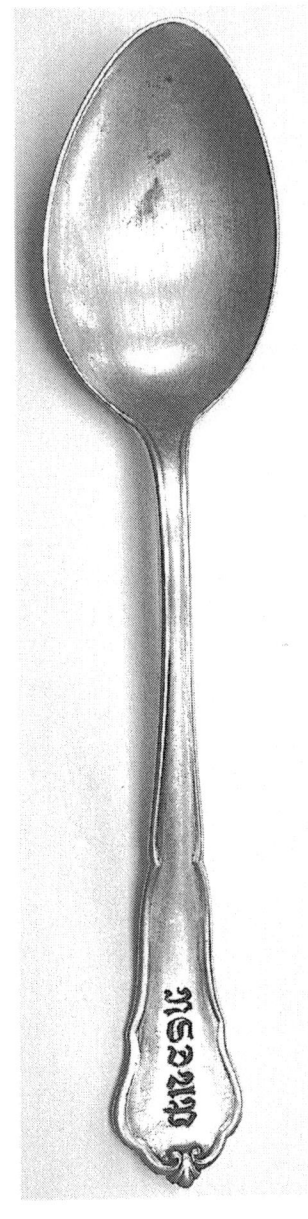

OG-19
L = 133 mm / 5 1/4"

OTHER GOVERNMENT

OG-19 'NSDAP'.
Nationalsozialistische Deutsche Arbeiterpartei

Teaspoon. Spoon carries NSDAP in Fraktur print on the obverse. Maker marked on reverse: Crescent moon, crown, '800' and 'HTB' for Hanseatishe Silberwarenfabrik, Bremen.

National Socialist German Workers Party: Founded in 1919 as the German Workers Party (DAP), the name was changed to NSDAP in 1920. Under the NSDAP, the National Colors (Reichsfarben) were Black, White and Red. The early NSDAP slogan: Deutschland Erwache - Germany Awake.

Fraktur Trivia: The first FRAKTUR typeface was designed when Holy Roman Emperor Maximilian (1493-1519) had the new type (German Script) created. It remained popular in Germany into the early 20th Century. On 3 January 1941, Martin Bormann issued a circular letter to all public offices which declared FRAKTUR (and its corollary, the Sutterlin- based hand writing) to be Judenlettern (Jewish letters) and prohibited its further use. ie the spoon predates 3Jan41.

A second explanation from Maik Kopleck's BERLIN 1933-1945, "its use was forbidden by a decree issued by Bormann on Hitler's order because in the annexed territories it had led to confusion." Surprisingly, the letterhead of Bormann's decree was in Fraktur type!

56

OG-20
L = 141 mm / 5 9/16"

OG-20 'NSDAP'

Teaspoon. High Leader's spoon, The obverse carries a Swastika surrounded by oak leaves - (Eichenlaub or EL), a symbol of strength. End is squared. Maker marked on the reverse: Crescent, crown, 800 GR for Gebruder Reiner, Krumbach Bayern. Founded 1914,

NSDAP Promise of Loyalty - I promise loyalty to my Fuhrer Adolf Hitler. I promise to always meet him and the leaders he will determine for me with respect and obedience.

Symbolism of: Oak Leaves = Spirited Struggle
Palm Leaves = Victory

58

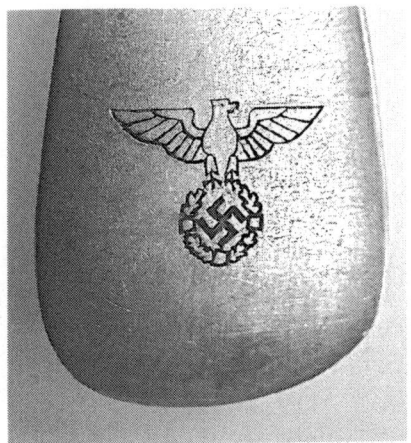

OG-21
L = 211 mm / 8 1/4"

OG-21 **NSDAP/SA**

Tablespoon. This aluminum tablespoon's eagle is looking to its left shoulder which symbolizes the Nazi party and was called the Parteiadler. In the absence of any specific organizational emblem, it is appropriate to assign it to either the NSDAP or the SA. Unidentified maker mark "C&C.W. 40".

In 1929, Hitler described the SA man as, "The SA attracts the militant natures among the Germanic breed, the men who think democratically, unified by a common allegiance.,"

OG-22
L = 145 mm / 5 3/4"

OG-22 'SA'

Teaspoon. The spoon carries the stylized "SA" monogram on the obverse. Maker marks: reversed "R" facing 'R' of Rossdeutscher & Reisig of Breslau, with crescent, crown,' 800'.

Sturmabteilung (German for "Storm Department", usually translated as "stormtroop(er)s)" The SA was the first paramilitary organization of the NSDAP - the German Nazi party. These were the "brown shirts". From its inception in 1921 till its demise in 1945, there were less than 200 men that occupied the top three positions in the SA. At its height in August 1934 there were some 2.9 million members. The SA was also the first Nazi paramilitary group to develop pseudo-military titles for bestowal upon its members. The SA ranks would be adopted by several other Nazi Party groups, chief among them the SS. The SA was very important to Hitler's rise to power until they were superseded by the SS after the 'Night of the Long Knives' of 30 June 1934 when the leadership of the SA were purged.

The SA motto: Alles Fur Deutschland - Everything for Germany.

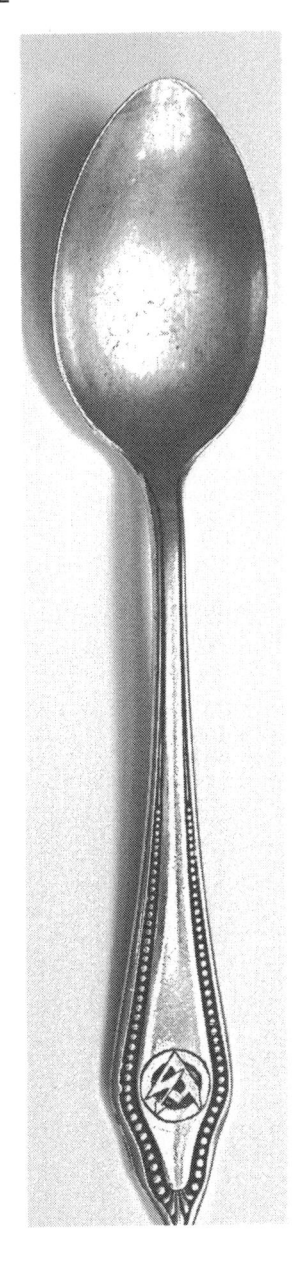

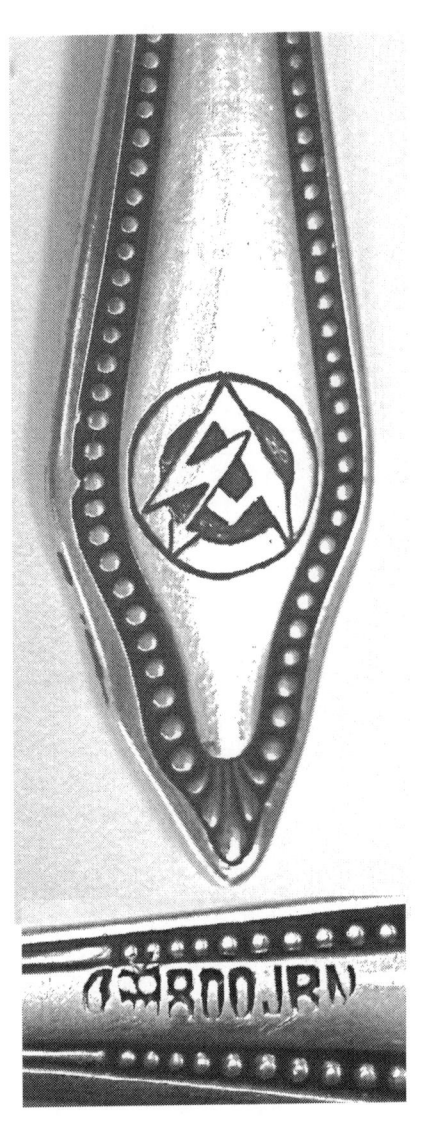

OG-23
L = 143 mm / 5 5/8"

OG-23 'SA'

Teaspoon. The spoon carries the stylized "SA" monogram on the obverse. Reverse marked with crescent, crown,'800'. Maker mark 'JRN' not identified

The Sturmabteilung abbreviated SA, (German for "Assault detachment" or "Assault section", usually translated as "stormtroop(er)s"), It played a key role in Adolf Hitler's rise to power in the 1930s.

SA men were often called "brown shirts", for the color of their uniforms, and to distinguish them from the Schutzstaffel (SS), who wore black and brown uniforms (compare the Italian black shirts). Brown colored shirts were chosen as the SA uniform because a large batch of them were cheaply available after World War I, having originally been ordered for German troops serving in Africa.

In 1930, to ensure the loyalty of the SA to himself, Adolf Hitler assumed command of the entire organization and remained Oberster SA-Führer for the remainder of the group's existence to 1945. The day to day running of the SA was conducted by the Stabschef SA (SA Chief of Staff). After 1931, it was the Stabschef who was generally accepted as the Commander of the SA, acting in Hitler's name.

Favorite sayings: "Terror must be broken by terror", and "All opposition must be stamped into the ground"

OG-24
L = 132 mm / 5 3/16"

OG-24 'HJ', Hitler-Jugend

Teaspoon. Hitler Youth Leaders spoon, Maker marked: crescent, crown, 800.

The HJ existed from 1922 to 1945, the 2nd oldest paramilitary NAZI group founded one year after the Sturmabteilung (SA) and attached to the SA. In July 1926 The Hitler-Jugend Bund der Deutschen Arbeiterjugend (Hitler Youth, League of German Worker Youth) received its final name. The HJ was banned in April 1932 by Chancellor Bruning but Chancellor von Papen lifted that ban in June 1932. The HJ diamond was adopted as the organizations emblem in 1933 along with its colors of Red and Black.. Membership became compulsory in December 1936. By 1945, the Volksturm commonly drafted 12 year old HJ members into its ranks for the defense of the fatherland. HJ motto: "Blut Und Ehre - Blood and Honor. Notable slogans: "Live Faithfully, Fight Bravely, and Die Laughing!" and "We were born to die for Germany!"

> **Hitler Youth Oath** - In the presence of this blood banner which represents our Fuhrer, I swear to devote all my energies and my strength to the savior of our country, Adolf Hitler, I am willing and ready to give up my life for him, so help me God.
>
> HJ Trivia: During the Battle of Berlin, The Reich Youth Leader (Reichsjugenfuhrer), Artur Axmann formed the HJ into a major part of the defense commencing at the Seelow Heights. General Weidling ordered Axmann to disband the HJ combat formations but in all the confusion his order was never carried out.

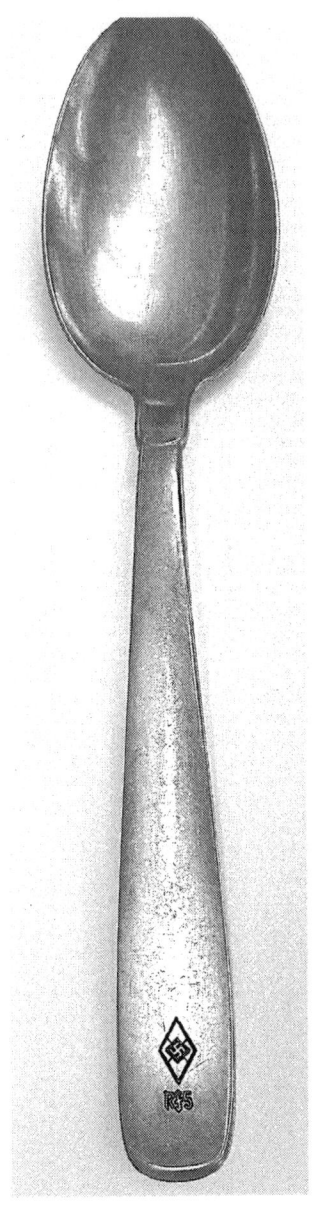

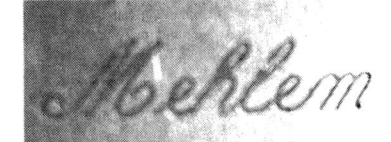

OG-25
L = 213 mm / 8 6/16"

OG-25 **HJ/RFS**

Hitler Youth "Reichsfuhrerschule (National-Leaders-School)

Tablespoon. This is something I have tried to avoid which is buying sets when I am focused on spoons. In this case, the niche was too tempting as this set is from a Hitler Youth "Reichsfuhrerschule (National-leaders-school) located in Mehlem, Germany. The obverse is stamped with the Hitler Youth diamond and swastika, beneath which is similarly impressed "RFS" for 'Reichsfuhrerschule". The reverse is stamped "Mehlem", being the location of one of the three HJ National Leaders schools - this one near Bonn, the others in Potsdam and for women, in Godesberg. The spoon and fork also have stamped to their reverses, higher up the handle and within horizontal rectangles, maker mark "Hanseat 90" the manufacturer's name, followed by the silver plate of "90" which is also impressed to the reverse of the knife's handle, at the top, and to the obverse of its blade, near its base, is faintly etched "NR" for "Nicht Rostend" or Not Rusting or stainless steel.

In addition to the traditional German school system, the Nazis established elite schools for the training of the young Nazis: the exclusive Ordensburgen (Order Castles) took the top graduates from earlier schooling and at a nominal age of 18 they were trained for another three years to be ready to assume high level positions in the Nazi Party.

68

REICHSARBEITSDIENST
1936

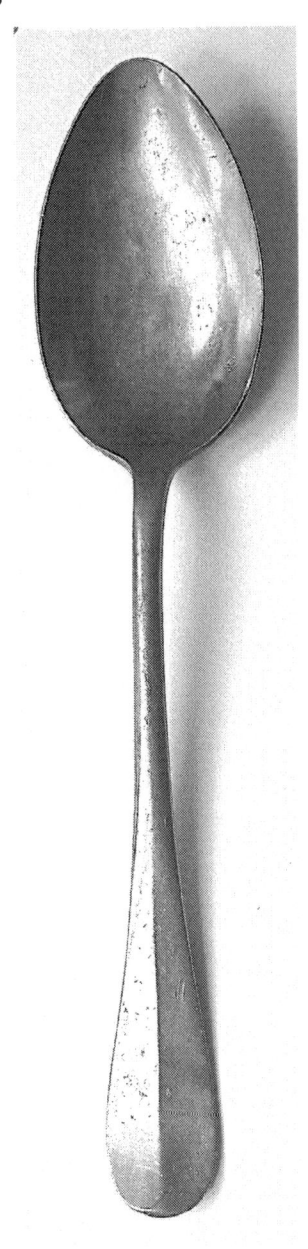

DURALIT ROSTFREI

OG-26
L = 217 mm / 8 9/16"

OG-26 '**RAD**'
"**Reichs Arbeitsdienst**" (National Labor-Service).

Tablespoon. This Mess Hall tablespoon (Essloffel). Marked on the reverse side with "REICHSARBEITSDIENST" "1936". Manufactured by Duralit and of stainless steel (Rostfrie).

RAD basis dates back to 1929's formation of AAD "Anhalt Arbeitsdienst" (Anhalt Labor-Service) and the FAD-B, "Freiwillingen Arbeitsdienst-Bayern" (Volunteer Labor-Service [of] Bavaria). In 1933, the NSDAP consolidated labor organizations into the NSAD, "Nationalsozialist Arbietsdienst" (National-Socialist Labor-Service); a national labor service. In June 1935, NSAD was re-designated RAD, in July RAD service became compulsory for both young men (prior to military service) and women, with all German citizens between 19 and 25 required to enlist for a 6 month term and military conscripts to serve 9 months. Typical work projects were road construction and farm labor.

The RAD motto: ArbeitAdelt - Work Enobles.

Note: A sub organization of NSDAP, the SDA - Schunheit der Arbeit (Beauty of Labor) which was established in 1934 and headed by Albert Speer, supplied canteens with flatware and cutlery.

70

OG-27 'DR', Deutsche Reichsbahn
(German National Railways)

Tablespoon and matching teaspoon from Hitler's private dining car, - The spoons obverse carries the "DR" logo, on the reverse the spoon is maker marked: Crescent moon, crown, 800, eagle of Bruckmann & Sohne., followed by a large '205' indicating it is from Sonderzug / Fuhrerzug car #10205 / #205.

This train pattern was used on the German National Railroad. Prior to 1939, Hitler's private train was labeled Fuhrerzug - Leader's Train. In 1939, Hitler's 1st Wartime Headquarters was established on the 17 car Fuhrersonderzug - Leader's Special Train. All coaches were specially constructed of welded steel and therefore weighing in at over 60 tons each. Hitler's private Pullman car was #10206 and fitted out to Hitler's own specifications. The car directly next to it was car 10205 (Hitler's private dining car with rose wood paneling) abbreviated as 205 on the car's china, flatware, silver serving pieces, and linens . The cutlery carries the Bruckmann maker's mark while, the porcelain was maker marked: Nymphenburg. The staff dining car was # 213. There were two full time silver polishers assigned to the Fuhrersonderzug! The train was code named "Fuhrersonderzug F' until 1940, then "Amerika" from a French town near Hitler's WWI location and finally "Brandenburg". His 206 Pullman car was blown up by German Army engineers in April 1945 on Hitler's orders.

OG 27 & 28
Tablespoon L = 211 mm / 8 5/16", Tea 140 mm / 5 1/2"

OG-28 "DR" Deutsche Reichsbahn

Details of Hitler's private dining car's silverware.

In 1924, the Deutsche Reichbahn was created as a state enterprise under the Reich Ministry of Transportation. On 10 Feb 1937, the Nazi government took total control of the rail network. To emphasize this, swastikas were added to the Hoheitsadler (sovereignty eagle) - the traditional symbol of Germany on all railcars, and the initials "DR" were held to stand for "Deutsches Reich" but were construed to be for "Deutsches Reichbahn. Maker marks identical to OG-27

Trivia: Hitler's Fuhrersonderzug sleeping carriage 10222 survived the war and was used by the President's of the Federal Republic of Germany into the 1980's.

74

OG-29 L = 216 mm / 8 1/2"

OG-29 **'DR'** Deutsche Reichsbahn

Table spoon from Goering's private dining car.

As with Hitler but on a grander scale, Herman Goering's two personal trains were in Obersalzburg in April 1945. His primary private dining car was number 10243 '243'. Other cars were '233', '234' and '244'. This tablespoon carries the Goring dining car number '243' and is maker marked: Capital 'B' (Bruckmann) with a locomotive symbol followed by a '90'. There have recently surfaced a number of the raised edge 243 spoons which are now the most prevalently available. The demonstrably different shape of this Goering spoon is evident when set side by side with the A. H. DR spoon and is generally described as with 'raised edge'.

Trivia: Goering's Sonderzuge were first named Asien I and Asien II and later renamed Pommern I and Pommern II.

Note: I have recently seen DR cutlery marked 244 and identical in form to the Hitler 205 above.

76

OG-30
L = 210 mm / 8 5/16"

OG-30 'R.K', Reichs-Kanzlei.

Tablespoon. This table service (besteck) has the eagle facing to his right, legs apart on a static swastika in the double wreath with an 'R' on the left and on the right a 'K'. There is no Greek key design. The reverse carries the crescent moon, crown, 800 and Bruckmann eagle. This is official, silver Besteck, or flatware, from the **'New' Reich Chancellery** / (Neureichskanzlei, Interestingly, although Wellner's "AH" had only one eagle, the Bruckmann's "RK" had both "Straight Wing" and "Swept Wing" (spread) eagles.

This was Hitler's Berlin chancellery and one of his official residences where all the most important state affairs were conducted. When present, Hitler used his formal 'AH' pattern, (see PS-1) otherwise, only the likes of Mussolini, Ciano, Chamberlain, Goring, Goebbels and Himmler used this flatware when the Fuhrer himself was not seated. Probably 100 times more rare than the 'AH' formal pattern. Considered a museum piece as the Chancellery was destroyed by fire in 1945 and afterwards occupied by the Russians so that very little survived. Shown here with a companion fork.

RK trivia: The cost of construction was estimated to be $ 100 million equivalent to $ 1 billion today. Hitler was very impressed when Speer managed both the design and had it constructed in a few days shy of one year by coordinating multiple construction teams working in parallel. The classic of "Nazi Architecture".

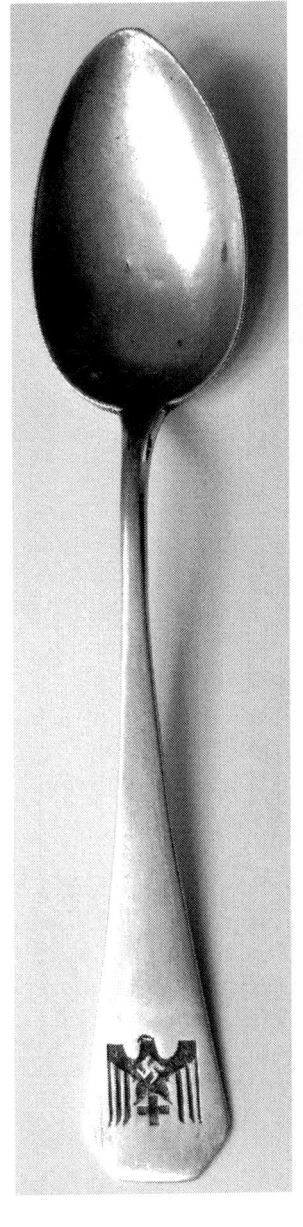

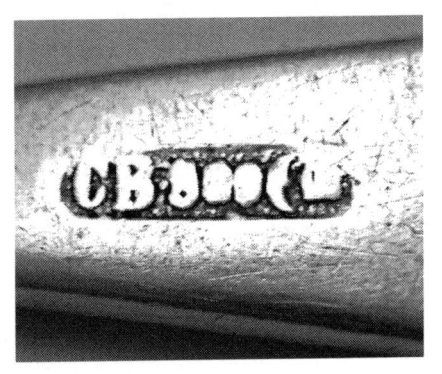

OG-31
L = 136 mm / 5 6/16"

OG-31 'DRK'.
Deutsches Rotes Kreuz (German Red Cross)

Teaspoon. The spoon carries the DRK logo on the obverse and maker marked on the reverse: "CB 800" with crescent moon & crown.

Originally a voluntary civil assistance organization started in 1864. The NSDAP recognized the DRK in December 1937 and took control in 1938. During the Third Reich, the DRK emblem had a black eagle with elongated down swept wings and a white, mobile swastika superimposed on its breast, clutching a red Balkan cross (known in English as a Greek cross - a cross with straight lines) in its talons while the standard international red cross flag was also still utilized to denote first aid and medical locations.

DRK Trivia - typical of Nazi protocol, daggers were a standard item of dress. Due to its noncombatant status, the DRK had to conform to the international Geneva convention which directed that members not carry any weapons, including edged weapons. As a result, the DRK 'Subordinates Hewer', introduced in 1938, was designed with a squared blunt tip and blunt scabbard to preclude its classification as a weapon and allowed its wear in the field. The DRK Leaders dagger, with a pointed tip and pointed scabbard, was classified as a weapon and could only be worn as a dress dagger, when not in the field.

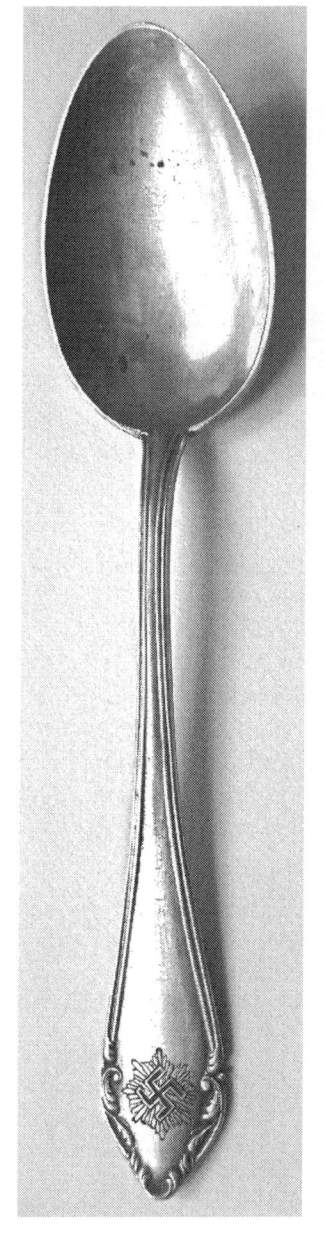

OG-32
L = 142 mm / 5 10/16"

OG-32 'RLB'.
National Air Raid Protection League

Teaspoon. This spoon carries the mobile swastika in an ornate sun burst background as illustrated in Brian Davis's 'Badges & Insignia of the Third Reich', plate 34, item #16 and is identified as the second pattern used by the RLB. Maker marked: undecipherable, '800', crescent moon, crown.

Reichs Luftschutzbund (National Air Protection League) Originally formed in late 1932, the Deutscher Luftschutzverband (German Air Protection League) was a voluntary organization designed to provide civil air raid protection in large civilian centers. In 1933 it was placed under the supervision of Hermann Goering's Reichsluftfahrt Ministerium (National Air Ministry). On 29 April 1933 the DLB was redesignated the Reichs Luftschutz Bund (National Air Raid Protection League) or RLB, now responsible for all aspects of civil air raid defense. Voluntary up to June 1935 - when obligatory service was established.

82

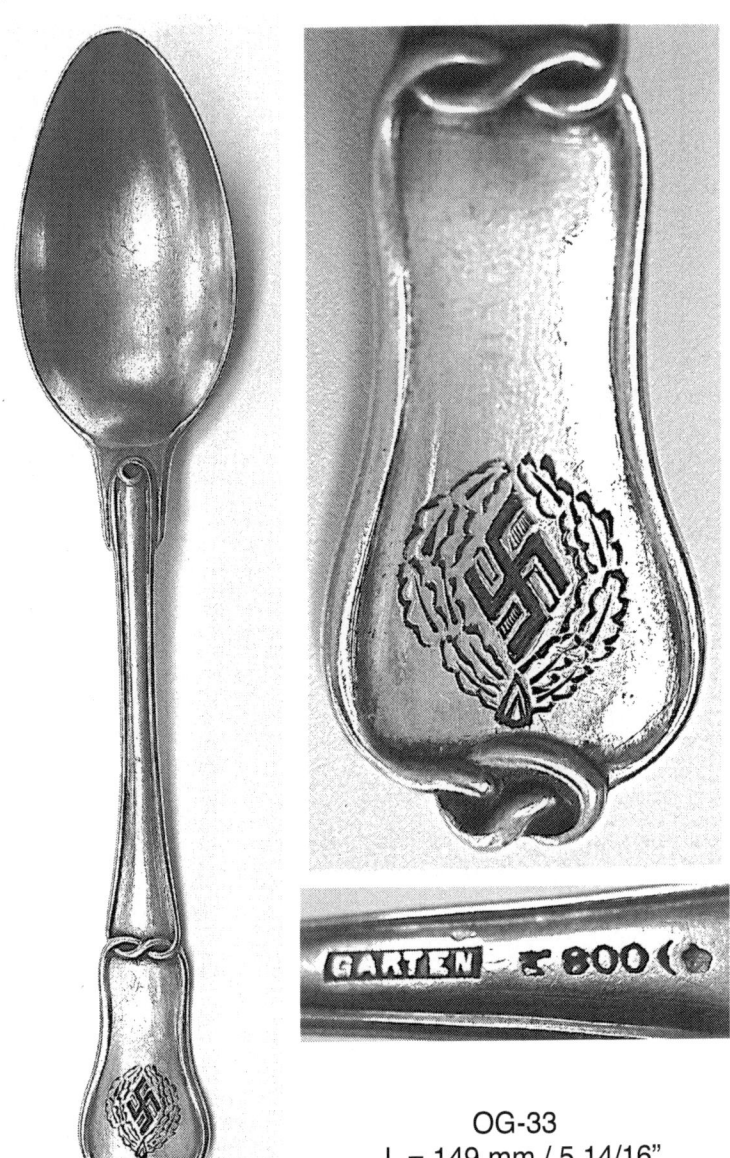

OG-33
L = 149 mm / 5 14/16"

OG-33 National-Socialistische Deutsche Studenten Bund - NSDStB
(National Socialist Student Federation)

Teaspoon. This teaspoon carries the Studentenbund Ehrenzeichen (Student Federation Decoration) on the obverse The reverse is maker marked 'GARTEN' 800 crescent moon, crown. This decoration has no eagle . The NSDStB emblem has the eagle clasping their elongated swastika as per the Sport Shirt Patch photo below. There is also a stylized initial H on the reverse as per below.

All German students at the universities were required to belong to the Studentenschaft (Student Corps). The Student Corps was responsible for making the students conscious of their duties to the Nazis state, and was obliged to promote enrollment in the SA and labor service. Physical training of students was the responsibility of the SA. Political education was the responsibility of the National-Socialistische Deutsche Studentenbund (NSDStB), (National Socialist German Student Bund) and was the Nazi "elite" of the student body and responsible for the leadership of the university students, and all leaders of the Student Corps were appointed from its membership. The Nazi Student Bund was solely responsible for the entire ideological and political education of the students.

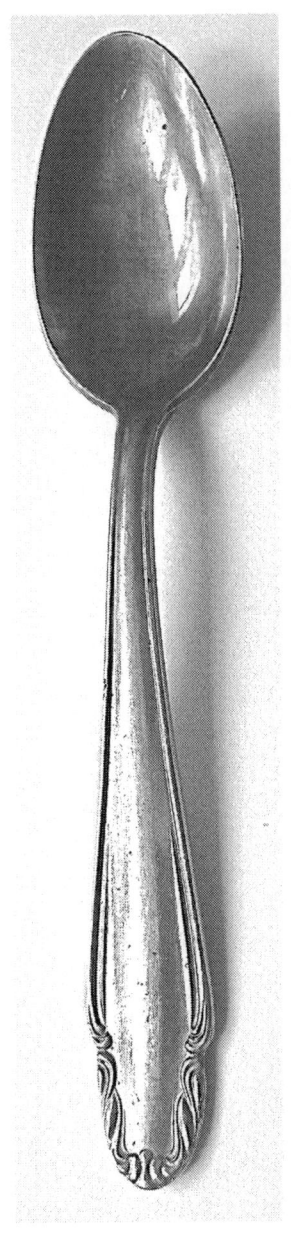

OG-34
L = 141 mm / 5 9/16"

OG-34 **Eagle**

Teaspoon. The eagle on this teaspoon's reverse faces to its right (a State organization) over '1942' with maker mark of the Manufacturer's name 'Mangasil' of Solingen with trade mark.

The National Emblem - (Hoheitsabzeichen) was the eagle and swastika of the NSDAP and later Nazi Germany.

Regarding the German Eagle: Per Wikipedia, "The Nazi party used the traditional German eagle, standing atop of a swastika inside a wreath of oak leaves, When the eagle is looking to its left shoulder, it symbolizes the Nazi party and was called the Parteiadler. In contrast, when the eagle is looking to its right shoulder, it symbolizes the country / state / military (Reich) and was called the Reichsadler." After the Nazi party came to power in Germany, they forced the replacement of the traditional version of the German eagle with their modified party symbol highlighting the swastika throughout the country and all its institutions.

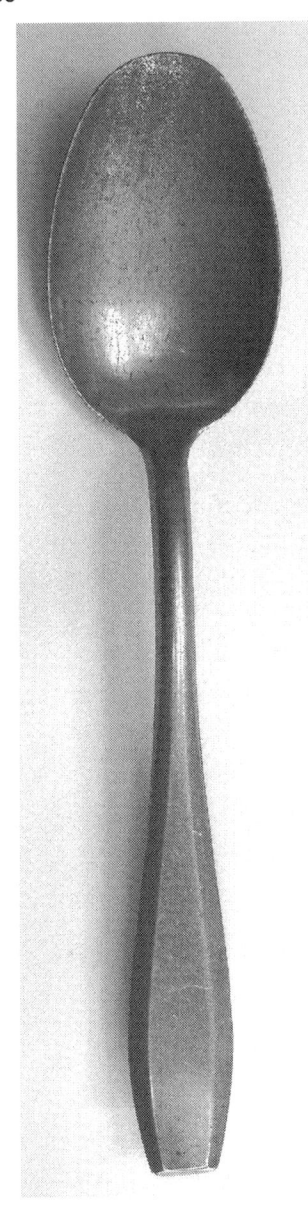

W-35
L = 212 mm / 8 5/16"

Wehrmacht
(Armed Forces)

W-35 HEER (Army)

Mess Hall Tablespoon (Kantine Esloffel) Roughly 8 3/8" long, natural aluminum alloy. Handle obverse is flat. The reverse of the handle is well marked with an impressed national eagle with outstretched wings and the manufacturers initials "W.S.M." and dated "42".

German Military Oath - 2Aug34 - "I swear by God this holy oath, that I will render to Adolf Hitler, Fuhrer of the German Reich and People, Supreme Commander of the Armed Forces, unconditional obedience, and that I am ready, as a brave soldier, to risk my life at any time for this oath".

In 1933, prior to Hitler's election, the Army had 100,000, by 1 October 1934 it was 240,000. By 1 Oct 1935 - 300,000. On 1 April 1938 the German Army was 28 divisions and by Autumn, including reserves, it numbered 55 divisions.

88

W-36
L = 210 mm / 8 1/4"

W-36 HEER

Mess Hall Tablespoon, Aluminum with raised central rib on obverse. Reverse handle maker marked "E100" and "WH" indicating Wehrmacht (Armed Forces), Heer, (Army). Plus an owner's? initial "W" scratched on reverse.

Trivia: To appreciate the pre 1943 logistics of a German Infantry Division, per "The German Infantry Handbook' by Alex Bucher - the 12th Infantry Division in the Eastern campaign from 22 June to 31 Dec 1941, a strengthened division of 20,000 men and 5,500 horses consumed 8,110 tons of food and fodder plus 15,100,000 cigarettes, 98,000 liters of alcohol, 6,516 kilo of chocolate etc The eastern campaign started with 99 Infantry Divisions and quickly built up to 119!

90

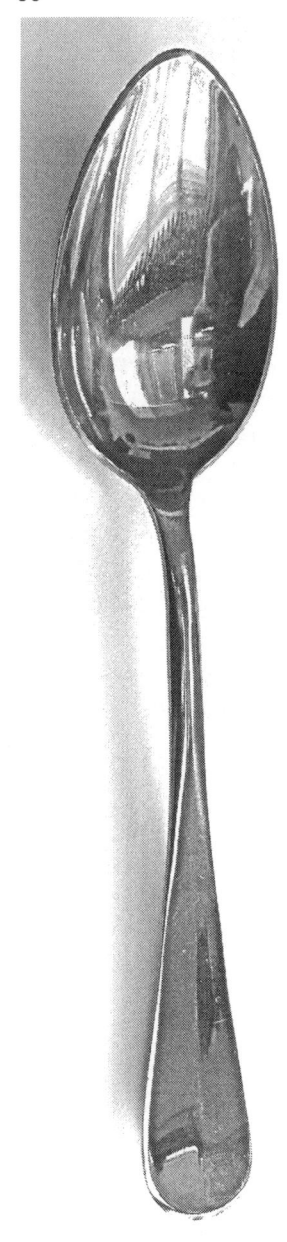

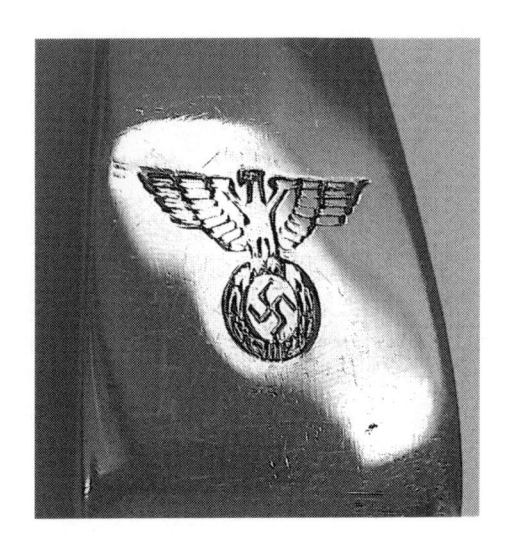

W-37
L = 209 mm / 8 1/4"

W-37 **HEER**

Tablespoon. Mil Issue, aluminum 8 1/4" long. The obverse of the handle has a raised central rib while the reverse carries a manufacturers mark "LGK&F" over 39 and the eagle.

Trivia: Due to manpower shortages and a scarcity of reserves, by the Spring of 1942, German forces in the East had 'absorbed' some 700,000 former Red Army soldiers, including an estimated 6,000 officers and former commissars. Ultimately, more than one million former Red Army soldiers would serve with the Germans. These Soviet citizens that volunteered to be unofficially employed as manual laborers and/or as German Army combat reinforcements were called HiWis for Hilfswillige "volunteer auxiliary' and within the military totaled some 250,000 in 1943 and were officially permitted to the level of 15% of divisional strength. In the East: as of Oct 1943 the German Infantry Division of 16,860 was reduced to 11,317 Germans and 1,455 HiWi's a reduction of 28%. In Dec 1944 a further reduction was made to 11,211 Germans and 698 HiWi's.

92

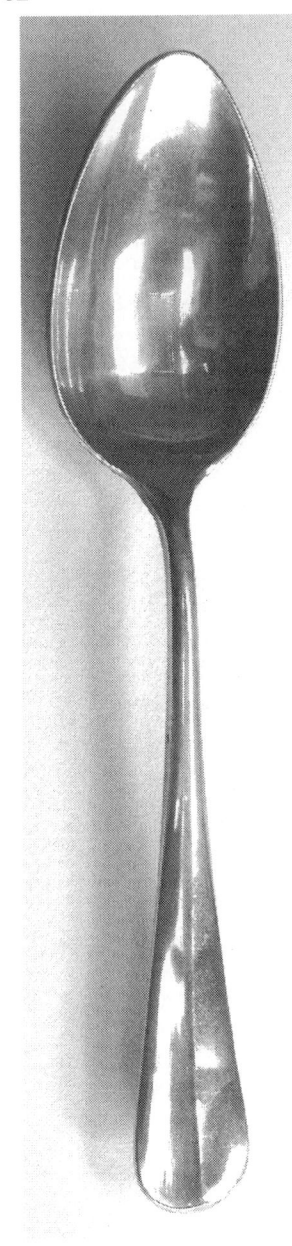

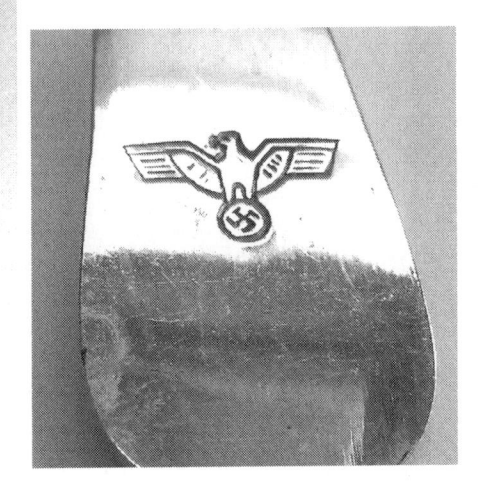

W-38
L = 139 mm / 5 1/2"

W-38 **HEER**

Demitasse spoon. Alloy with a central raised rib on the obverse and maker marked "B.A.F. N. 39" with eagle facing right on a mobile swastika on the reverse side. Identical style to M-23

> Fact: WWII Campaigns length: Poland 27 Days, Denmark 1 Day, Norway 23 Days, Holland 5 Days, Belgium 18 Day, France 39 Days, Yugoslavia 12 Days, Greece 21 Days.
>
> Blitzkreig? German Infantry Divisions typically relied on their 5,000+ horses to supply 80% of their motive power. Consuming 22 pounds of fodder daily, required some 55 tons of fodder daily per division. For the Polish campaign, the 197,000 horses required 135 railway trucks of fodder daily. Of the 3 million horses and mules enlisted by the German Army between 1939 and 1945, more than 1.7 million perished. These numbers do not include the smaller Panje horses of the East which were used in large numbers but were not officially recognized by the military.

94

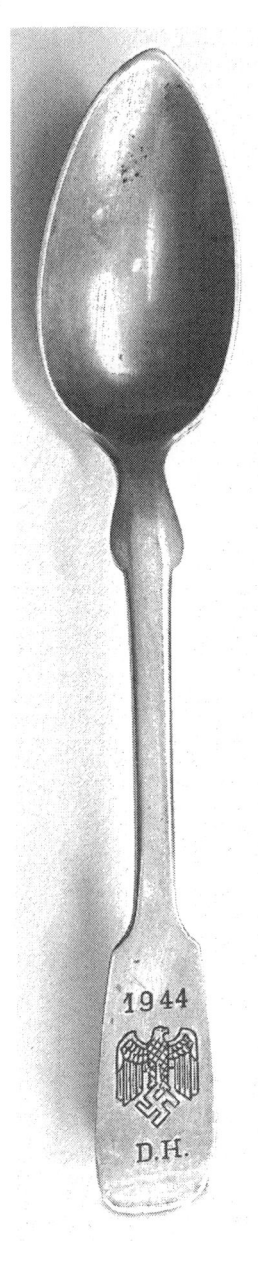

W-39
L = 142 mm / 5 10/16"

W-39 **HEER**

Teaspoon. **1944** over **Eagle** looking to his left over **D.H.** (Deutsches Heer - German Army). Marked with crescent moon, crown, 800, 'N' (Possibly Ludwig Neresheimer, Hanau, founded 1890)

Dated cutlery tends to disappear by 1943 when "Advancing on All Fronts" was a bitter memory and Germany suffered some 1,686,000 casualties that year.

Fact: Of the 13,600,000+ that served in the German army from 1939 to 1945, some 4,200,000+ were killed or missing in action. Total German losses in the Eastern Campaign from 1941 to 1944 alone were 1,400,000+ killed in action with an additional 1 million missing in action.

96

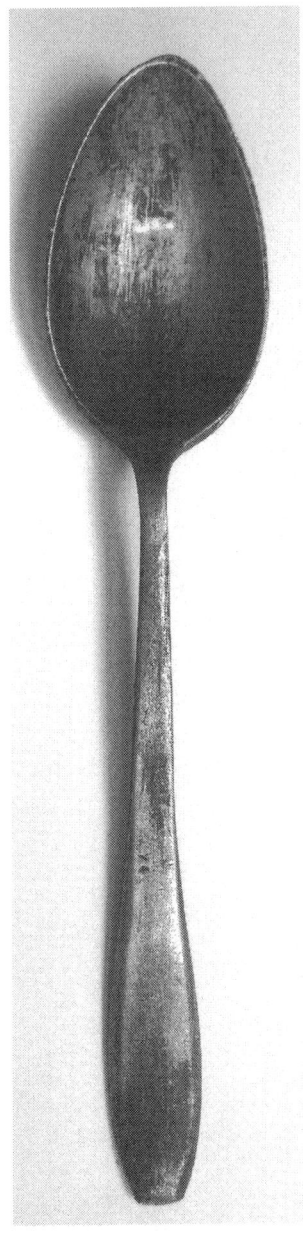

W-40
L = 153 mm / 6"

W-40 Heer

Teaspoon. Marked with "H. U." on the obverse. H.U. is the short form for Heeres Unterkunft (Army Quarters / Billets) This spoon appears to be a 'dug' item with heavy corrosion but caries the Heer eagle looking right with no makers mark. The material is undetermined but indicates a late war product as does the workmanship.

In 1933 Germany had a 100,000 man Military as prescribed by the Treaty of Versailles in 1920. The Wehrmacht (armed forces) was founded on 15Mar35 and the German military was expanded to 3,343,000 in 5 years under Hitler. The Wehrmacht on 1Sep39 had 3,180,000, (with 2.7 Million heer./army). Maximum strength achieved was 9.5 Million under arms with 5.5 Million in the Heer and at 9 May 1945 some 7.8 Million were still under arms with 5.3 Million Heer. Heer typically accounted for 75% of the Wehrmacht and within the Heer, 82% were Infantry Divisions.

98

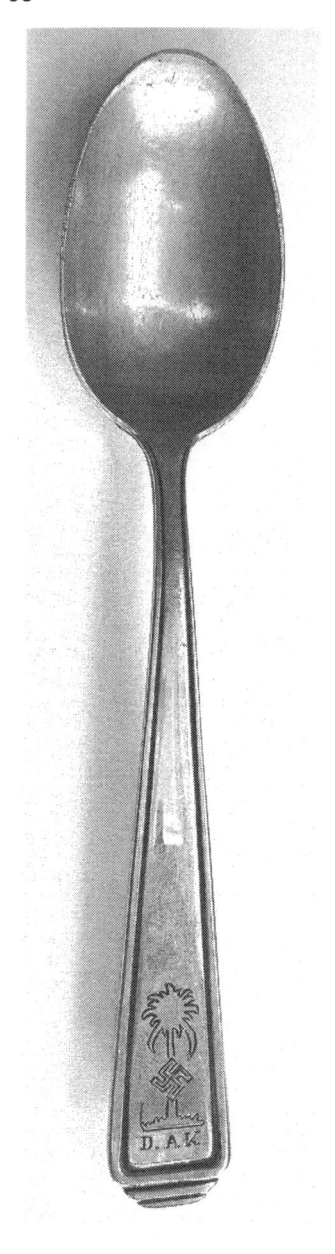

W-41
L = 145 mm / 5 11/16"

W-41 D.AK,

das Deutsches Afrikakorps (The German Africa Corps)

Teaspoon. Marked with DAK logo with maker mark 'AWS' in a squared box (August Wellner & Sohne), The AWS maker mark was used by Wellner from 1928 to 1941, 800, crescent moon and crown.

The D.AK was formed on 12 Feb 1941 as the original German expeditionary force in Libya and Egypt during the North African Campaign of World War II. Its original mission was to act as a blocking force in Libya and Tunisia to support the routed Italian army group which was under great pressure by the British forces.

100

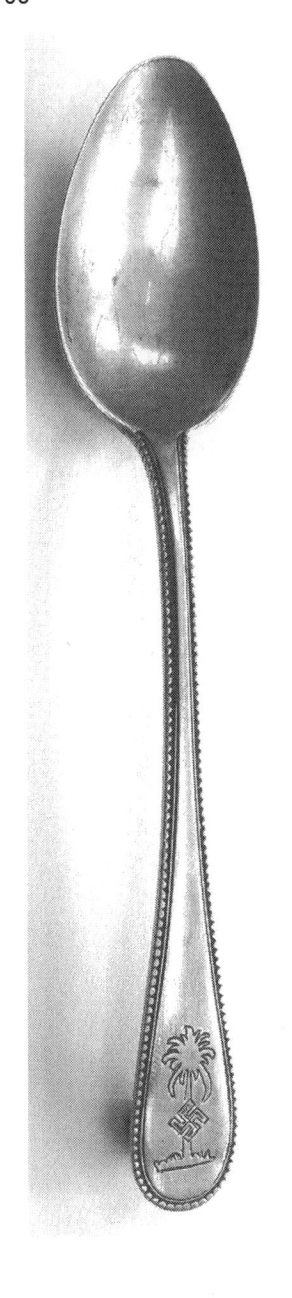

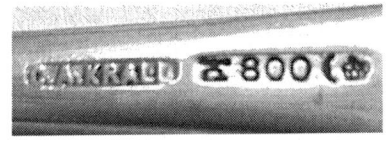

W-42
L = 144 mm / 5 11/16"

W-42 **D.AK**,

Teaspoon. **das Deutsches Afrikakorps** marked with D.AK logo. Small dots surround the top handle of the spoon. Maker marked C.A. Krall, 800, crescent moon and crown.

Rommel's AfrikaKorps required 70,000 tons of material monthly to operate but typically received much less. On 13 May 1943 the remnants of the Afrikakorps surrendered in Tunisia having suffered some 12,808 killed in action. By this time, the D.AK transport vehicles were predominately made up of captured British trucks.

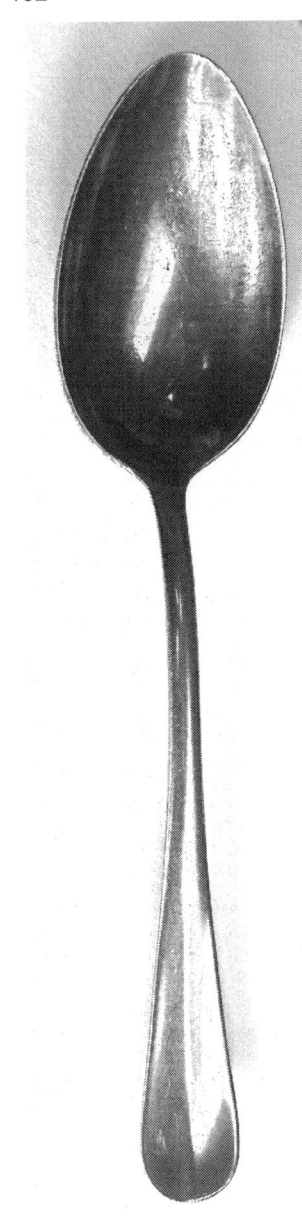

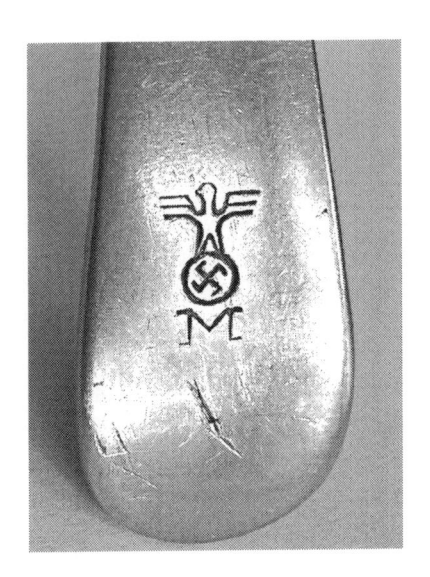

W-43
L = 212 mm / 8 3/8"

W-43 KREIGSMARINE (KM)

Tablespoon. **(Navy) Mil Issue**, stainless steel with raised spine on obverse. On the reverse the manufacturers initials, 'HHL' for (Heinrich Haupt Ludenscheid Besteckfabrik) in an octagonal border, "ROSTFREI' with KM logo of a simplified eagle over a mobile swastika in a circle over the 'M'.

Fact: From the Versailles Treaty strength limitation of 15,000 personnel, over 1,500,000 served in the KM, with some 65,000 killed in action

Note: The Navy appears to be the least interested in the incorporation of the Nazi symbols and their renderings show it.

104

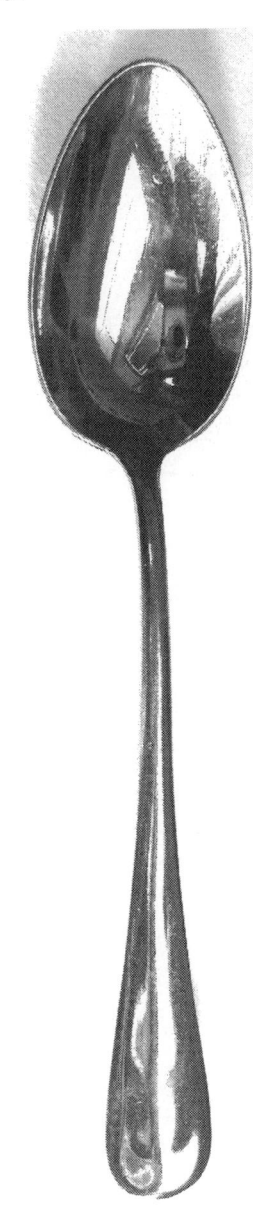

W-44
L = 144 mm / 5 11/16"

W-44 **KREIGSMARINE**

Teaspoon. (Navy) Mil Issue with raised spine on obverse. On the reverse the makers mark is a circle divided diagonally by crossed swords with a letter 'V' at the top, letter 'D' on the left and a letter 'N' on the right with a letter 'S' at the bottom, the maker mark for (Vereinigte Deutsche Nickelwerke AG Schwerte) followed by 'BLANCADUR'* and at the bottom of the spoon the Kriegsmarine symbol with the 'M' in bold double outline.

> *Blancadur identifies the process of Blancadur Rhodium electrolyte deposition of pure rhodium to achieve a brilliant extremely bright and glossy surface layer.

106

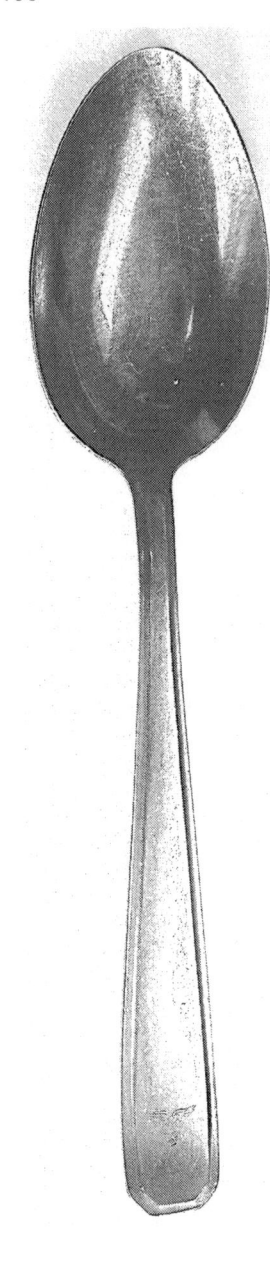

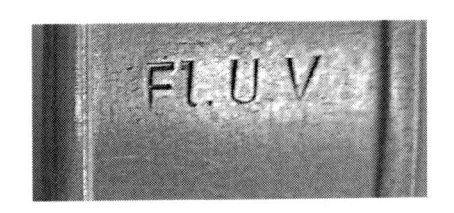

W-45
L = 206 mm / 8 1/16"

W-45 LUFTWAFFE

Tablespoon (Esloffel), **(Air Force) Mess Hall** Roughly 8" long, one piece stainless steel. The obverse of the handle is marked with a faint, impressed early style "droop tailed" Luftwaffe eagle. The reverse of the handle is well marked with impressed manufacturers initials "CH" for (Chromolit) and date "41", followed by "Rostfrei" (Rust Free). At the end of the handle, stamped crosswise are the initials, "Fl.U.V." indicating, Flieger Unterkunft Verwaltung (Flight Barracks Administration)

> The Luftwaffe is considered to be a child of the Nazi party. Under the Versailles Treaty of 1919, Part V, Germany was forbidden from having any military air organizations.
>
> The Luftwaffe was officially recognized by Hitler on 9 March 1935 when he called for volunteers to serve in the German Air Force.

108

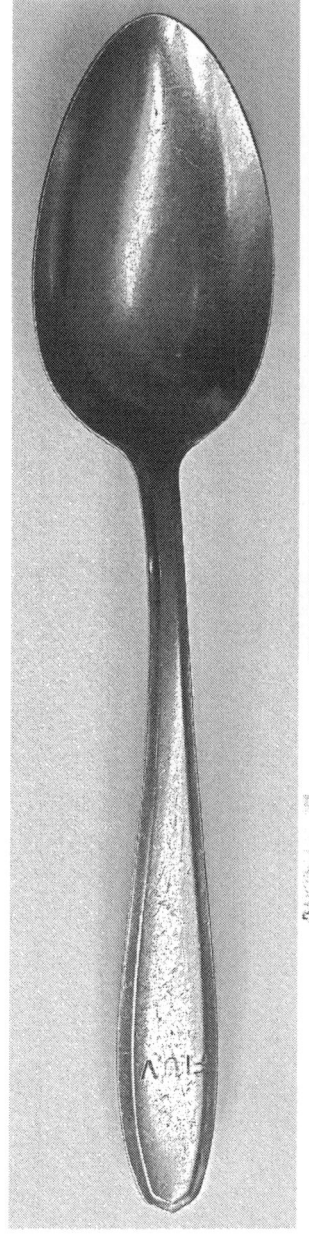

W-46
L = 210 mm / 8 1/4"

W-46 **LUFTWAFFE**

Tablespoon, mess hall stainless steel. Obverse of the handle is well marked with impressed initials "Fl. U.V." indicating, Flieger Unterkunft Verwaltung, (Flight Barracks Administration). Manufacturer's name "Oxydex", logo of a 4 leaf clover in a square and "rustfrei" is impressed on the reverse. The FlUV is impressed upside down.

Luftwaffe Trivia: Luftwaffe field divisions were rapidly mobilized from Luftwaffe ground personnel, from Oct 42 to early 1943 some 200,000 Luftwaffe personnel were organized into 21 Field Divisions - organized as 7,000+ strong M1942 Rifle (Jager) Divisions to replace the massive loss of men on the Eastern front. Due to the lack of training and poor performance in the field, of the 21 divisions formed, 17 were either destroyed or disbanded before the end of the war.

W-47   L = 209 mm / 8 1/4"

W-47 LUFTWAFFE

Tablespoon with raised, early Droop-Tailed Eagle (1935/6) and swastika on obverse. Maker marked reverse: Roman numeral 'II' and a diamond enclosing crossed swords and the letters "V' at the top of the cross, 'D' on the left, 'N' on the right and 'S' below the cross, the maker mark for (Vereinigte Deutsche Nickelwerke AG Schwerte) Probably silver plate.

Germany's front line fighter plane was the Messerschmitt Bf 109 with direct fuel injection as opposed to the Spitefire's carburetor engine which gave the Messerschmitt significant advantages in certain maneuvers. The kill ratio (almost 9:1) made this plane far superior to any of the other German fighters during the war and over 33,000 were produced. The closest rival was the Focke-Wulf Fw 190 with a kill ratio of 4:1, but introduced later in the war when things were more difficult. Some 20,000 Fw 190's were built. These two aircraft were half the total aircraft manufactured by Germany in WWII.

112

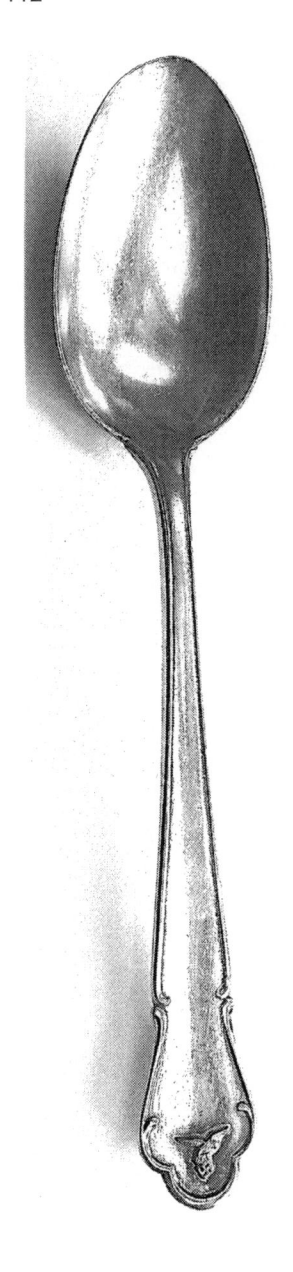

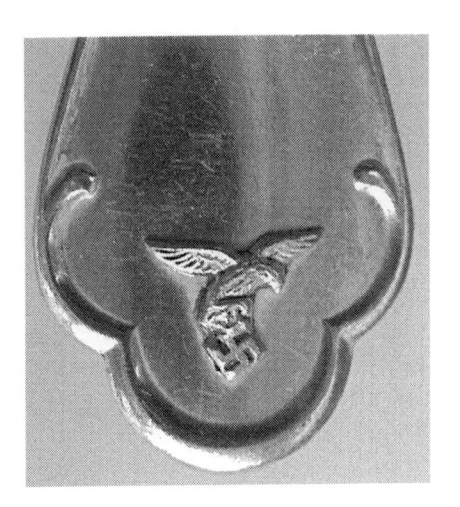

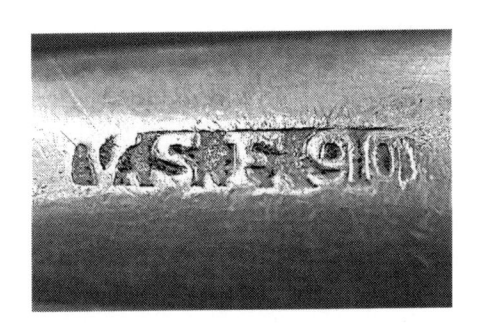

W-48
L = 207 mm / 8 1/8"

W-48 LUFTWAFFE

Tablespoon. **Officers Service**, in silver plate with raised, early Droop Tailed Eagle and gold plated swastika on obverse. Maker marked on reverse: V.S.F.90

> Fact: Of the 3,400,000 that served in the Luftwaffe during the period 1935 to 1945, some 165,014 were killed in action including 70,000 aircrew.

114

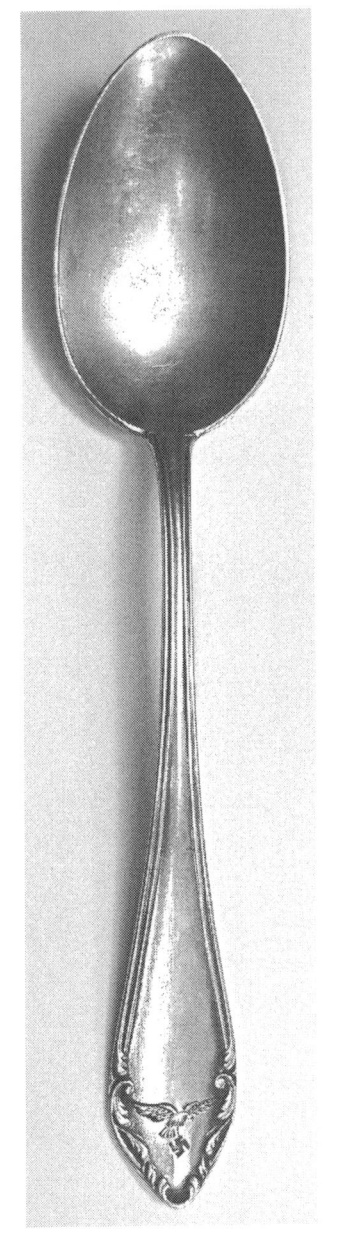

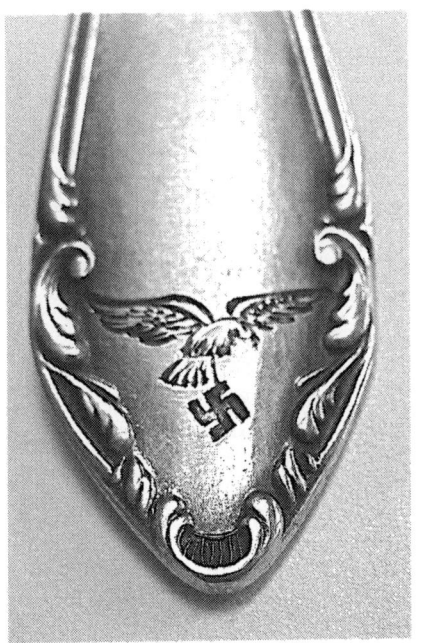

W-49
L = 142 mm / 5 10/16"

W-49 Luftwaffe

Teaspoon. Officer's service piece. Marked on obverse with Luftwaffe emblem. Reverse unidentified maker mark followed by 800 crescent moon and crown.

Maximum air strength in Europe during WWII: Germany 5,000 combat aircraft, America 21,000, England 8,500 and Russia 17,000.

German WWII FIGHTER aircraft production rates:
    1939   37/ month.
    1940   126/ mo
    1942   250/ mo under Udet, (Nazi Germany's shortest General)
    1943   1,000/ mo under Milch
    Fall 1944 2,500/ mo under Speer

116

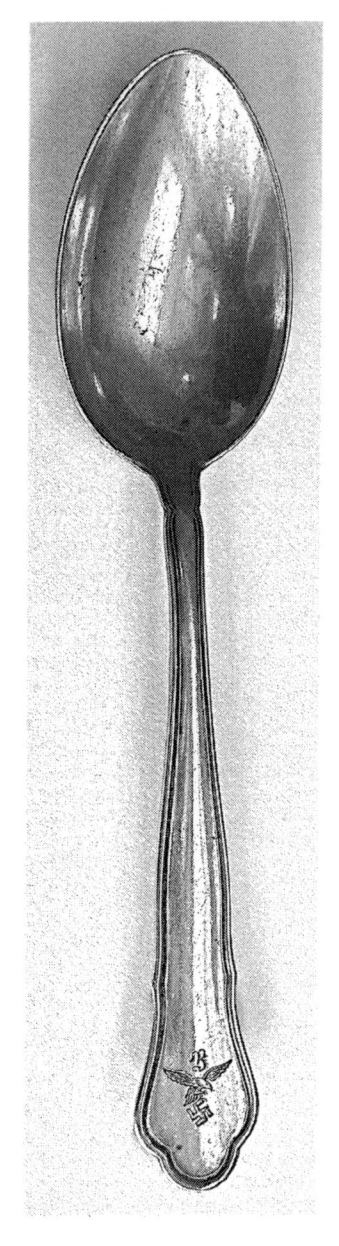

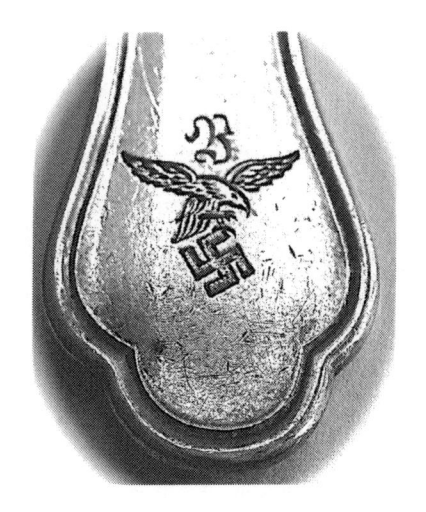

W-50
L = 174 mm / 6 13/16"

W-50 LUFTWAFFE

Dessert spoon. General Officers Service in silver with a fraktur personalized? letter "B" over the Luftwaffe Eagle on the obverse. The reverse is well marked with the manufacturer's name 'LAMEYER' followed by the national mark (reichsmark) of a crescent moon & crown (Halbmond und Krone) and 800 (the decimal silver standard mark) followed by a maker's mark of a small 'W' left of a capital 'L' followed by a '&' and a capital 'S' with a crown on the top. The "W" for the first name of Wilhelm, the 'L' for family name Lameyer, the '& S' most probably for 'and son' of Hanover .

Total German Aircraft production: 113,515 aircraft with 100,000 destroyed and 70,000 aircrew killed.
　　(The US produced over 100,000 aircraft in 1944 alone of a total 300,000)

　　Note: The English teaspoon holds 5 ml, a dessert spoon 10 ml and the tablespoon 15 ml.

SS

An explanation as to the plethora of SS Besteck comes from an item in a Germania International write-up: "Traditionally, in Germany, tableware was the gift of choice. This involved sets of spoons, knives and forks sometimes in special cases. There was born a tradition in the Waffen-SS of presenting table ware to couples who were about to be married. This went back to the 1930's with the Allgemeine-SS. From 1939 on thousands of war wounded of the Waffen-SS had nothing to do other than lie around in hospital beds or languish about with no actual mental therapy. The SS command decided that various artistic projects should be offered to them that would fill the bill. The question was what therapy would give the recuperating soldier something to occupy his hours, and at the same time be something that would add to the cultural expression and acumen that was always the professed agenda of the SS. Then someone came up with the idea of supplying the men with simple tools for constructing various items such as presentation dinnerware and also engraving tools and applique kits were supplied for acid etching and hand engraving. The men were allowed to sell these hand tooled gifts. One of the most popular of the art projects was making up sets of dinnerware--knives, forks, spoons--with the SS symbols applied. The actual flatware was not produced by these wounded men, rather it was a matter of certain companies who produced these utensils to donate them to the soldiers who, with their newly acquired tools, applied carefully the SS runic symbols to the various pieces. Firms such as Krupp, Sy and Wagner, Tiger, Eickhorn, Wellner etc., donated sets from vendor stocks to be decorated and sold with the benefits going to the soldiers families.

These were often called wedding sets because SS men of various Waffen-SS units would often give them as presents to a comrade and his wife as a marriage present. It became a respected tradition among the ranks of the Waffen-SS and continued on to the end of the war." With over 900,000 serving in the Waffen-SS, and over 400,000 wounded in action, this was a large number to find distractions via the Verwundete (wounded) Program!

Legal Problems for the SS

Due to its creation by Hitler personally and its subsequent involvement with the NSDAP as a Party-affiliated organization, the SS was listed as a criminal organization at Nuremberg in 1945. The Waffen-SS (the militarized formations of the SS was named Waffen-SS in the winter of 1939-40 having originally been formed as the SS-VT or SS (Special Troops) was thus denied the rights of the other military service veterans. Only conscripts sworn in after 1943 were exempted from criminal charges on the basis of involuntary servitude. All Allgemeine-SS members were listed as criminals.

The SS mottos: Meine Ehre Heisst treue -
                        My Honor is Loyalty
                                &
                        Believe! Obey! Fight!

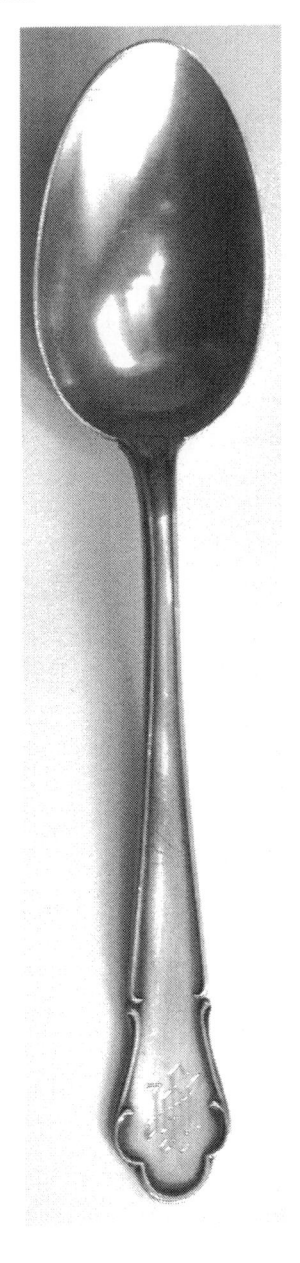

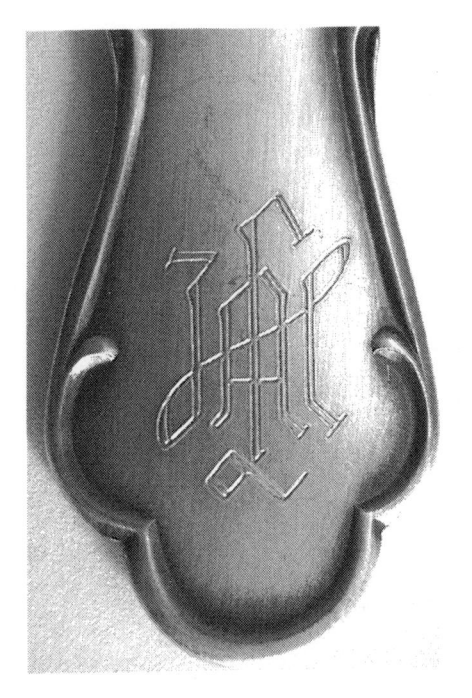

SS-51
L = 208 mm / 8 3/16"

SS-51 1st SS Panzer Division 'Leibstandarte Adolf Hitler'

Tablespoon. **Liebstandarte SS Adolf Hitler.** This is a formal pattern (also referred to as 'twisted wire' pattern) of intertwined LAH letters as used in the barracks of the SS-Leibstandarte Adolf Hitler, the elite soldiers of the Schutzstaffel, or Black Corps.

Raised in September 1933, the original LSSAH compound was located in South West Berlin at the Lichterfelde Kaserne (Berlin-Lichterfelde) which was an old Prussian cadet training school and became the headquarters for Hitler's body guard regiment, the Leibstndarte-SS "Adolf Hitler". Later became the headquarters for the SS-Panzer-Division Leibstandarte under 'Sepp' Dietrich .

The spoon is in the Beidermeier pattern which evolved in such cities a Vienna, Munich and Berlin during the 'Bieddermeier' period of 1815 - 1848 in Germany and Austria. Maker marked 'V.S.F. 90'.

122

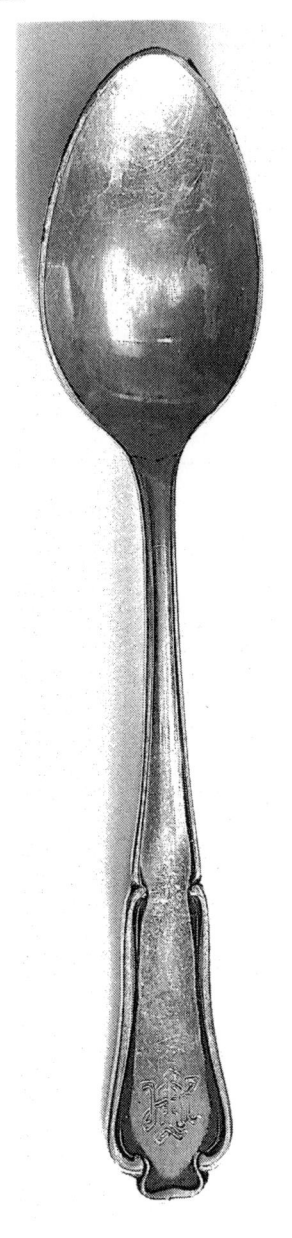

L = 144 mm / 5 11/16"

SS-52 **LSSAH**

Teaspoon. Intertwined script letters L-A-H. Sometimes referred to as twisted wire design. Maker marked "Becker 90".

This premier Waffen-SS Panzer Division was formalized on the 10th anniversary of the Beer Hall Putsch on 8 / 9 November 1933, It was Adolf Hitler's original bodyguard / lifeguard unit, commanded by SS-Gruppenfuhrer Josef 'Sepp' Dietrich. Fought in Poland, Czechoslovakia, Holland, France, Yugoslavia, Greece, Russia, Belgium, and Hungary. Of the June 1944 strength of 19,700 troops, the remaining 1,500 survivors with 16 tanks surrendered to US troops in Austria in 1945.

Note: Track 16 of the 2005 digitally re-mastered "Triumph of the Will" DVD of the 1934 Nazi Party Rally in Nuremburg filmed by Leni Riefenstahl has some 5 minutes of the LSSAH review accompanied by their band playing Hitler's favorite, the Badenweiler March with appearances by both Himmler and Sepp Dietrich.

124

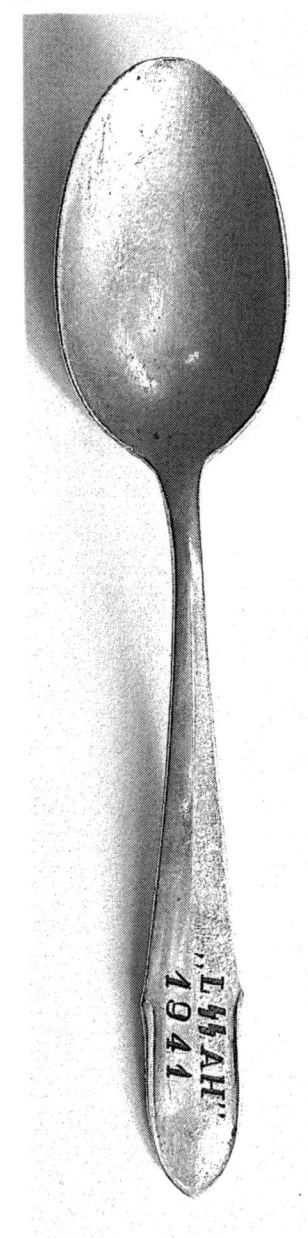

SS-53
L = 138 mm / 5 7/16"

SS-53 **LSSAH 1941**,

Teaspoon. Obverse marked "LSSAH" 1941. Reverse maker marked: WMF, (Wurttembergische Metallwarenfabrik of Geislingen, 1853 to the present) crescent, crown, 800.

SS Oath - Nov 33 - "I swear to you, Adolf Hitler, as Fuhrer and Reich Chancellor, loyalty and bravery. I vow to you, and those you have appointed to command me, obedience unto death. So help me God."

In 1929, Hitler described the SS man as, "Those who throng to the SS are men inclined to the authoritarian state, who wish to serve and obey, who respond less to an idea than to a man."

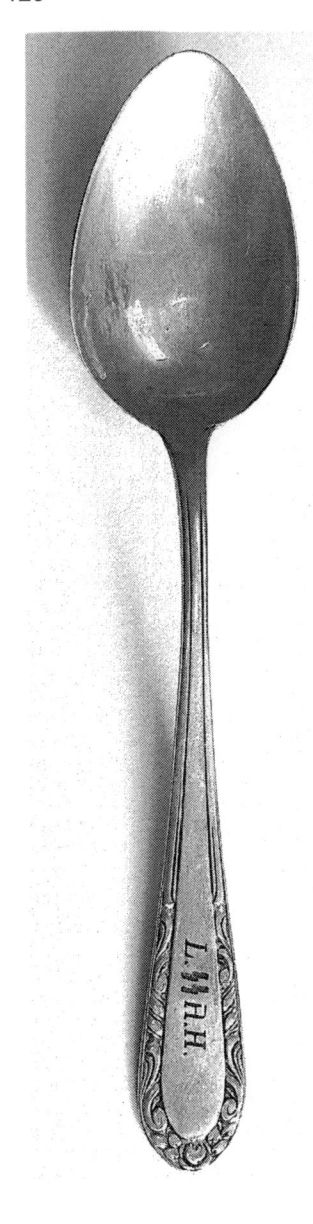

SS-54
L = 136 mm / 5 6/16"

SS-54 **LSSAH**.

Teaspoon. Obverse monogram: Capital 'L' , 'SS' runes, Capital 'A' and Capital 'H'. Maker marked on the reverse: 'Reichsmark' , 800, LW in a crest (Lutz & Weiss, Pforzheim founded 1882). Pattern: High relief , floral pattern, both sides, asymmetrical with roses at base.

In the early years prior to and of WWII, the Army resented the SS for taking the best candidates (volunteers) and as the Army controlled procurement for both, they took the best weapons first, supplying the W-SS with weapons from acquired / captured stocks.

Weapons fielded to each organization during those early years:

	Army	W-SS
Pistol	P.08 & P.38	Belgian High Power
Rifle	K98k Mauser	Hungarian 98/40 re-chambered
LMG	MG34 & MG42	Czech ZBvz26

.

128

SS-55
L = 140 mm / 5 9/16"

SS-55 2nd Panzer Division 'Reich'

Teaspoon. Obverse monogram SS-Reich, (originally established as the SS-V-Div in October 1939 with later name changes from the April 1940 designation as SS-Division Deutschland to October 1940's 2nd SS-Panzer Division "Reich" and in May 1942, after refitting with more tanks, assault guns and armored personnel carriers it was renamed SS-Panzer Division 'Das Reich'. Maker marked: 800, crescent moon, crown,unreadable entry, XX, for Wilhelm Muller of Berlin. Scalloped handle, double outline.

As a result of the occupation of Czechoslovakia in 1938 - 1939, Hitler was able to detail weapons acquired as: 1,582 airplanes, 2,175 pieces of field artillery, 469 tanks, 500 antiaircraft guns, 43,000 machine guns, 1,090,000 rifles, 114,000 revolvers, a billion rounds of ammunition and 3 million artillery shells in his 28 April 1939 Reichstag speech. Those MG's ended up in the W-SS. See the 3rd SS Panzer Division description on page 137.

130

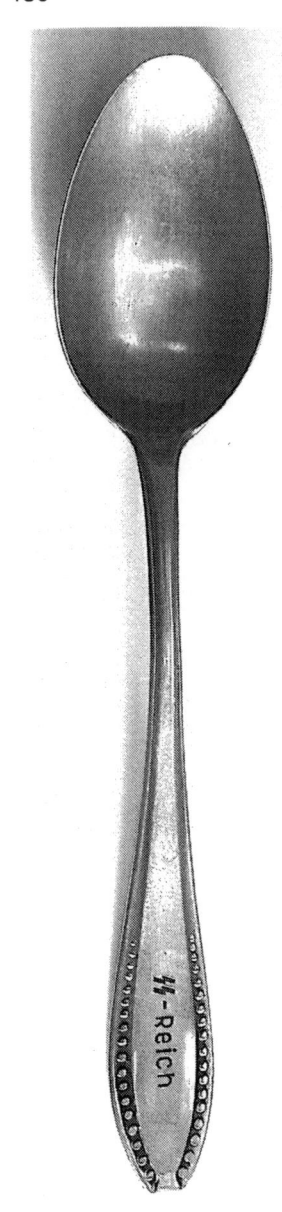

SS-56
L = 139 mm / 5 1/2"

SS-56 **SS-Reich**

Teaspoon. Obverse SS-Reich. Reverse hallmark: Reichsmark, "800", followed by unknown mark with "LSF" in an oblong enclosure. Pattern: bottom 1/ 3rd of obverse has 18 symmetrical dots of increasing size on each side with largest at bottom.

During 1939 and 1940, German forces occupied western European countries which allowed the W-SS to recruit pro-Nazi's, anti communists, Volksdeutsche etc. while the Wehrmacht was not authorized to do so. By the end of 1942, the W-SS fielded some 200,000 troops.

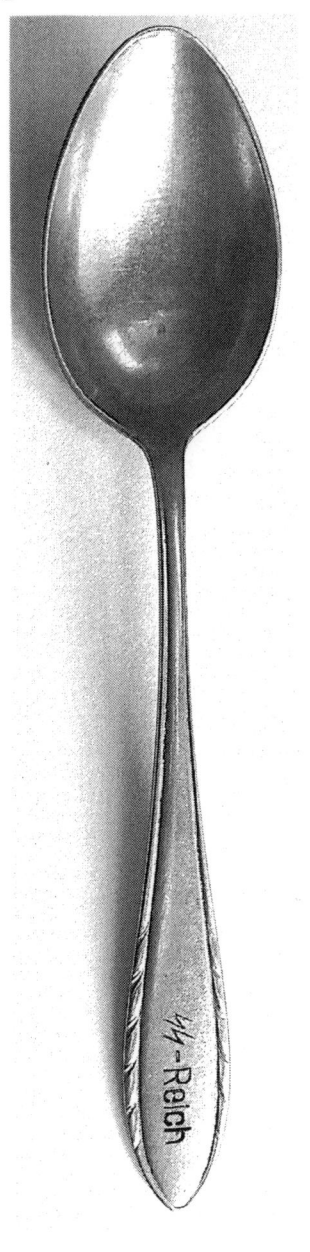

SS-57
L = 146 mm / 5 3/4"

SS-57 **SS-Reich**

Teaspoon. Obverse 'SS-Reich' with the SS in what is termed 'lightning bolt' style. Highlights on edges of lower 1/3. Reverse maker marked; Berndorf over their symbol of a 'bear' and Alpaca below in an overall oval shape.

SS enlistment requirements were 25 years for officers, 12 years for NCO's and 4 years for enlisted men. The Officer and NCO enlistment durations date from those specified by the Treaty of Versailles for the German Army in an effort to discourage enlistments.

134

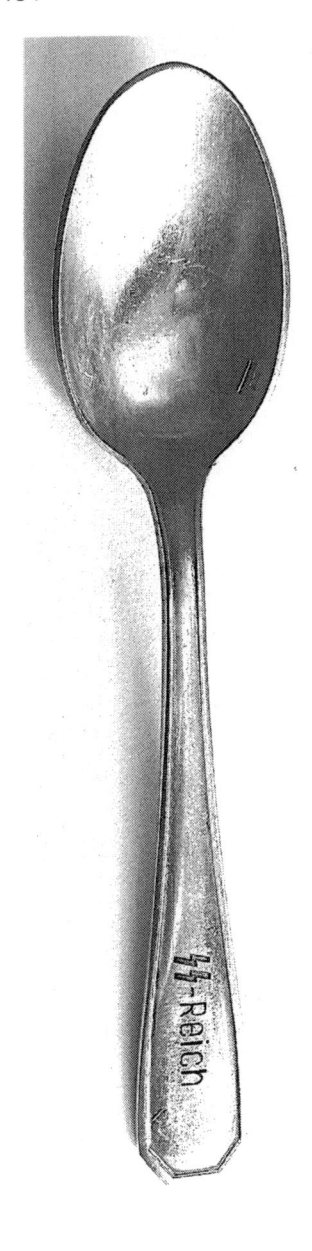

SS-58
L = 138 mm / 5 7/16"

SS-58 **SS-Reich**

Teaspoon, Obverse carries a textured SS - Reich. Reverse is unmarked.

On 5 Dec 1941, SS-Obergruppenfuhrer (4 Star) Paul Hausser, commanding SS Division 'Reich' came within 16 kilometers of the outskirts of Moscow, Temperature was -36C / -33F.

SS-Oberstgruppenfuhrer Hauser, whose nickname was "Papa Hauser" lost an eye in combat and became famous as, 'the SS general with the eye-patch'.

In 1946, Hauser stated. "The guards of the concentration camps and the personnel in the command did not belong to the Waffen-SS." See the 3rd SS-Panzer Div description on page 137.

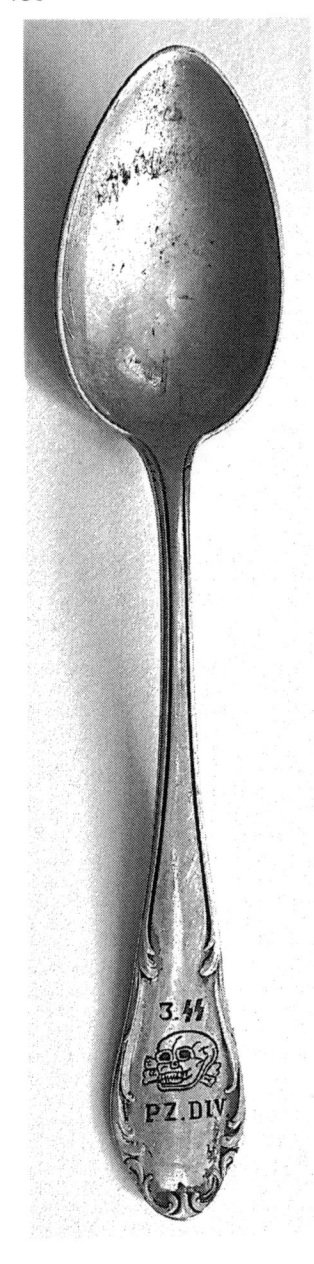

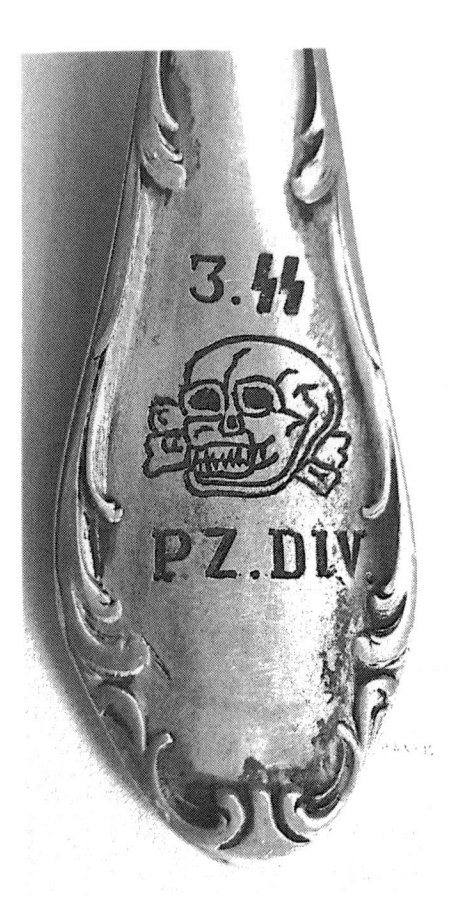

SS-59
L = 141 mm / 5 9/16"

SS-59 3rd SS-Panzer-Division 'Totenkopf' (Death's Head)

Teaspoon. Obverse carries the 3rd's coat-of-arms and reverse has the maker mark: E. Kludas, 800, crescent, & crown.

Raised Nov 1939 with most of the initial enlisted men coming from the SS-Totenkopfverbande, (SS Concentration Camp Guards). Through the Battle of France the division was generally equipped with ex-Czech weapons. - In November 1942, 'Das Reich', 'Totenkoph' and 'Wiking' were officially re-designated as SS-Panzergrenadier Divisions, and finally acquired the same type and quantity of equipment to that of army panzer divisions.

Surrendered to US troops in Austria 9 May 1945 with less than 1,000 men and 6 tanks from an original strength of 19,000. Handed over to the Russians

138

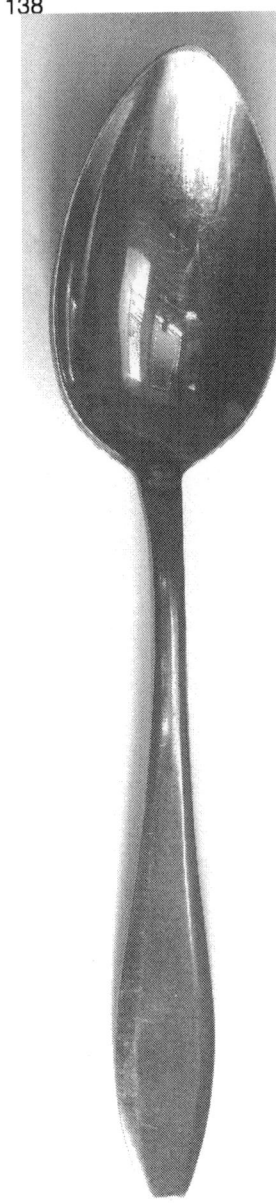

SS-60
L = 215 mm / 8 7/16"

SS-60 5th SS-Panzer-Division 'Wiking'

Tablespoon. Obverse is flat and unmarked. Reverse carries 'SS-Div. Wiking' & 'ROSTFREI', '

SS-Div. Wiking'. The 5th SS-Panzer-Division (Viking) was originally formed in November 1940 as the SS-Division (mot.) Germania by consolidating the regiments Germania, Nordland (Scandinavians), Westland (Dutch, Flemings) and the 5th SS-artillerie regiment into a new divisional unit. On January 1st 1941 the division was renamed, SS-Division "Wiking" and on November 9th 1942 the division was upgraded and renamed SS-Panzer-Grenadier-Division "Wiking". The division was upgraded again and received its final designation on October 22nd 1943 as 5th SS-Panzer-Division "Wiking" and surrendered in Furstenfeld, Czechoslovakia in May 1945. Although the enlisted men were predominantly Nordic volunteers, it was officered by Germans.

140

SS-61
L = 133 mm / 5 1/4"

SS-61 9th SS Panzer Division 'Hohenstaufen'

Teaspoon. Obverse carries the 9th's coat-of-arms. Reverse carries the crescent moon, crown 800 and maker's mark HTB for Hanseatishe Silberwarenfabrik, Bremen.

The Hohenstaufen, named after the family of the first German Emperors and specifically for family member Frederick Barbarossa whom the Fuhrer considered a great hero. Activated in early 1943 and faced with manpower shortages, 70 percent of the division's manpower were conscripts with 60% to 70% from the years 1925/26 or about 18 years of age. Included were a number of ethnic Germans from Hungary. In September 1944 strength reduced to 2,500 men or 20% of its original strength as a result of losses in France, particularly around Caen and Avranches..
Transferred to Western Germany in late September to be brought up to strength, their numbers were made up with Luftwaffe personal and other remnants. Participated in the failed Ardennes offensive, moved to Hungary and suffered severe losses against the Russians in March 1945 west of Budapest. Hitler was so enraged by their failure to defeat the Russians that he ordered the men of the 1st, 2nd, 9th and 12th Divisions of the Waffen SS to be deprived of their decorations and cuff bands. They fought their way back to Austria and on 5 May 1945 surrendered to US troops near Steyr.

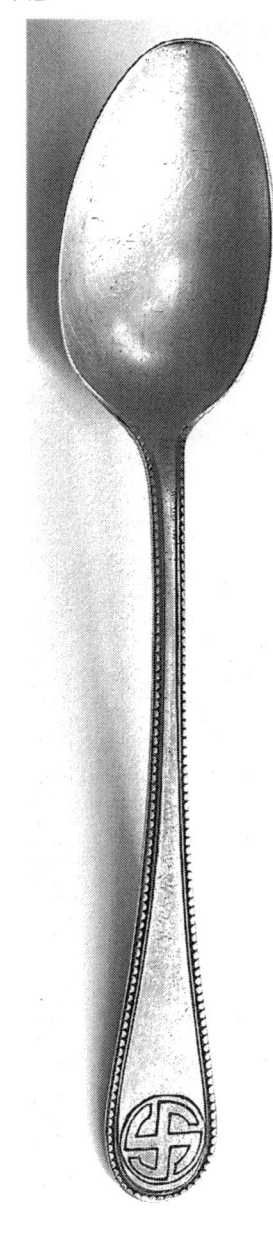

SS-62
L = 145 mm / 5 3/4"

SS-62 11th SS-Freiwilligen-Panzer-Grenadier-Division "Nordland'.

Teaspoon. Obverse carries the 11th's coat-of-arms. Reverse is maker marked: G H DANZIGER '800' crescent moon crown.

Formed in the summer of 1943 of various existing foreign volunteer units. The first SS Division to be officered by foreign volunteers. Most of the volunteers were from Scandinavia but the division had the widest range of nationalities found in a single German division including Danish, Hungarian, Dutch, Norwegian, Estonian, Finnish, French, Romanian, Spanish, Swedish, Swiss and British volunteers that had either served in the division or been attached to it.   Its emblem is the "Sun wheel" rune - a circular swastika. On 25 April 1945, the primary defender of the Reich Chancellery in Berlin was the SS Division Nordland with virtually no Germans. They had never taken a prisoner and did not expect to be made prisoners.

Motto: When all were unfaithful, we remained faithful.

Note: Along with Nordland, the other major defenders of Berlin were the 33rd W-SS Div Charlemagne (French) and the 15th W-SS Div (Latvian).

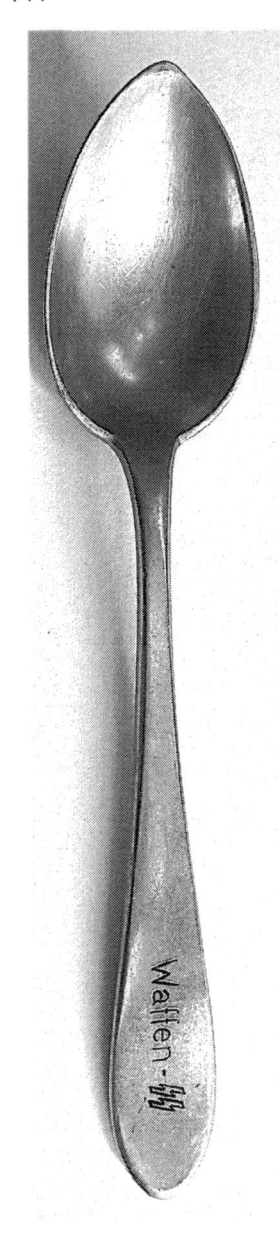

SS-63
L = 149 mm / 5 14/16"

SS-63 WAFFEN SS

Teaspoon. Obverse plain with no decoration marked 'Waffen-SS'. Reverse hallmarked with a Wellner's 'elephant' over 'Alpacca' enclosed in an oval.

Waffen-SS or Armed-SS, literally Weapons-SS was the combat arm of the Schutzstaffel and founded in 1939.

Waffen-SS consisted of 38 combat divisions, each with numerical designations followed by such names as "SS Panzer Division", "SS Panzergrenadier Division" and "Waffen Grenadier Division Der SS". The 3rd SS Panzer Division = "Soldiers of Destruction" and the 12th SS Panzer Division = 'Fighters not Soldiers". Waffen-SS KIA estimated at 180,000, WIA 400,000 and MIA 70,000.

Waffen SS Trivia: Although some 922,000 served in the Waffen-SS, ultimately 57 percent were non-German nationals! Breakdown: Reich Germans 400,000, West Europeans 137,000, East Europeans 200,000 and Volksdeutsche (ethnic Germans) 185,000. The so called 'Germanic' divisions were the 1st LSSAH, 2nd Das Reich, 3rd Totenkopf and the 5th Wiking.

146

SS-64
L = 133 mm / 5 1/4"

SS-64 SS.

Teaspoon. A formal pattern in art nouveau style. It seems to be heavily silver plated approximating the look of real silver. Reverse stamped: "P" "100". The SS runes may have been soldered in place. It is thought to be from the SS-Totenkopf division headquarters in the Bavarian Mountains (SS-Oberbayern).

Trivia: W-SS Divisions had no Division chaplain
In 1941 Heinrich Himmler was quoted, "I have six divisions composed of men absolutely indifferent in matters of religion. It doesn't prevent them from going to their deaths with serenity in their souls."

148

E. KLUDAS 800

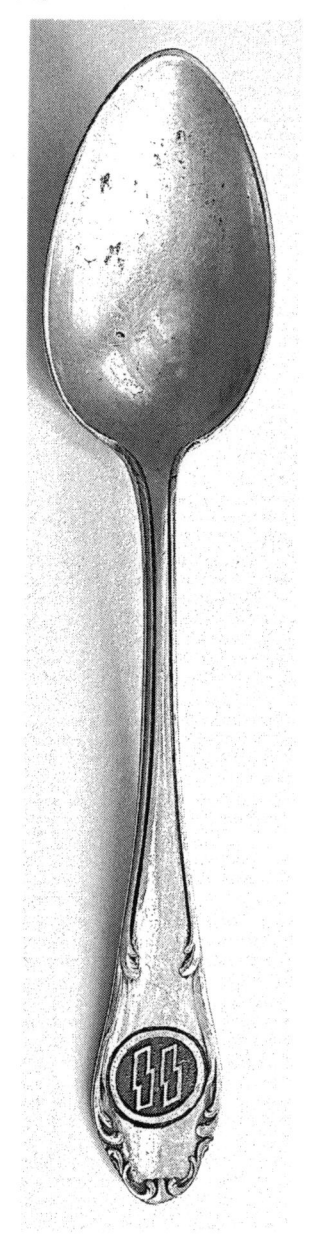

SS-65
L = 142 mm / 5 9/16"

SS-65 **SS**

Teaspoon. Obverse has the SS in a double circle with scolloped edges   Reverse maker marked: E. Kludas, 800 crescent moon, crown. The double circle was also seen on the saddle blankets of the SS equestrians as well as athletic sport shirts (sporthemd).

Note: When Germany took over the northern part of Italy on 8 September 1943 as the Italian Social Republic, the SS could accept Italian volunteers. Himmler forbid them the SS Sigrunen and the SS sleeve eagle. He required them to use Italian specific emblems such as a sleeve eagle clasping a fasces in its talons but they did wear the death's head cap emblems.

Trivia: The SS colors were black and white, the same as worn by the Teutonic Knights.

150

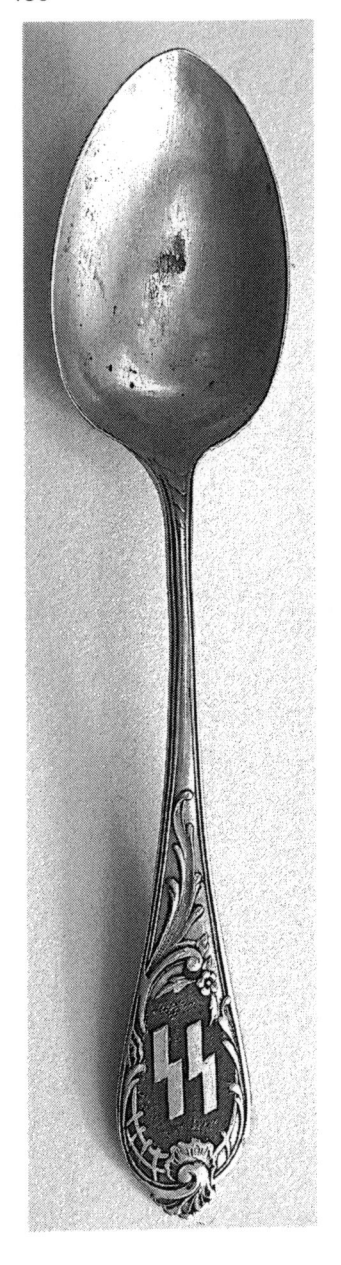

SS-66
L = 127 mm / 5"

SS-66 SS.

Mocha spoon. Obverse carries a very bold SS with high ornamentation. Reverse maker marked crescent moon, crown, 800, crossed hammers of Gebruder Petersfeldt of Berlin, founded 1848..

The Algemeine-SS or General-SS was order formed by Hitler in March 1923 as the Strosstrupp Adolf Hitler (Shock Troops Adolf Hitler) composed of 30 men. The NSDAP was banned after the 9 November Putsch. Released from prison in December 1924, in April 1925 Hitler formed a new bodyguard called the Schutzkommando which on 9 November 1925 became the Schutzstaffel (Protective Squad). Himmler was appointed the Reichsfuhrer-SS on 6 January 1929 and was granted, by Hitler, the status of an independent organization under direct control of the NSDAP, Nationalsozialistische Deutsche Arbeiterpartei, (National Socialist German Worker's Party) in July 1934.

152

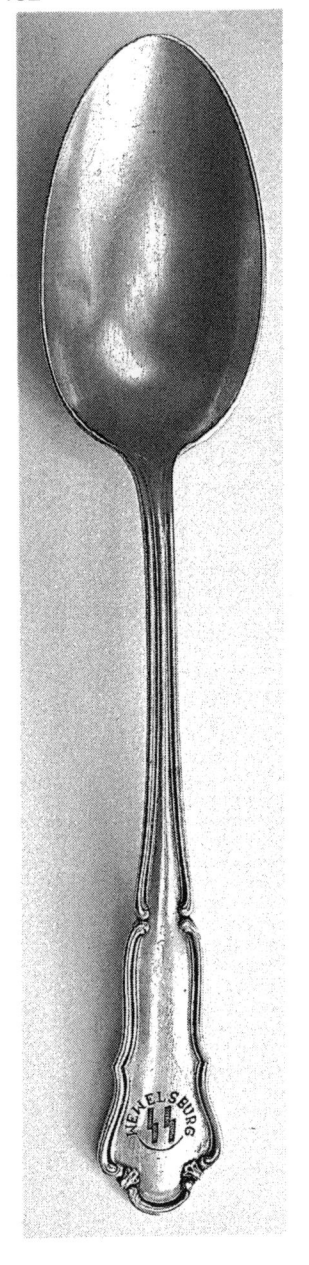

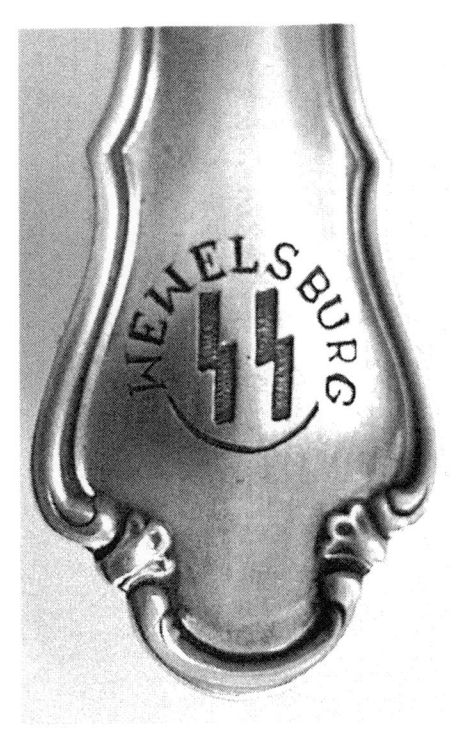

SS-67
L = 216 mm / 8 9/16"

SS-67 SS Wewelsburg,

Tablespoon Obverse carries the SS with Wewelsburg wrapped around the top and raised ribs, both sides, interrupted at 1/ 3 above bottom, two lobes. Reverse carries the maker mark of M. H. Wilkens, Bremen-Hemelingen, founded 1810 and still active) + 800 + Reichsmark.

On 27 July 1934 Himmler leased Wewelsburg castle for 100 years. The castle, one of only 3 triangular castles in the world, was to become the ritual headquarters of the SS Ordensburg und Reichsfuhrerschule (Cultural Relics and Leadership School) under the command of SS General Siegfried Taubert with a library of 12,000 volumes. SS honor rings of deceased SS elite members were to be returned. Himmler was to have been buried in the crypt. The spoon has been engraved, not stamped, leading to the possibility that this was done on site by "Niederhagen Labor Camp" ie concentration camp detainees as the smallest KZ or konzentracion camp collocated with the castle as a labor source. These silver pieces were only used in the North Tower by VIPs at this "Camelot of the SS". The castle was the venue of various Ahnenerbe-Forschungsund Lehrgemeinschaft - (Society for the Research and Teaching of Ancestral Heritage) ceremonies, the body for the research of ancestral heritage..

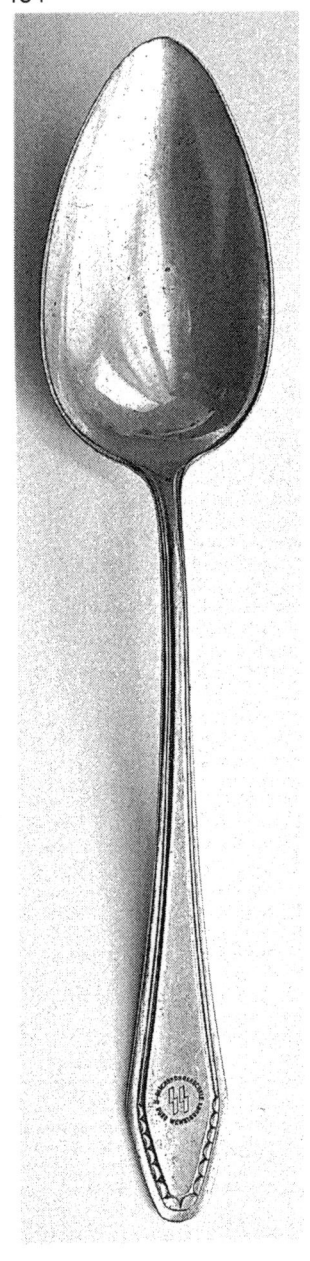

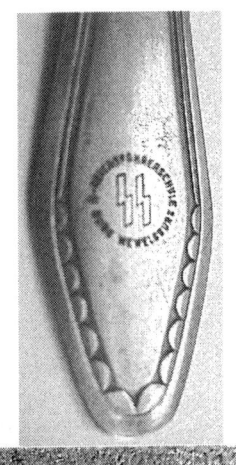

SS-68
L = 211 mm / 8 5/16"

SS-68 SS/RFS

Tablespoon. Obverse carries the SS-Reichsfuhrerschule (SS-National Leaders School) at Wewelsburg emblem.. Reverse maker marked: A Centaur (an unknown maker mark) with a "20" on a square.

Himmler intended that Wewelsburg should ultimately be used as a Reichshaus der SS-Gruppenfuhrer or SS Generals' Residence, but with the outbreak of the war, it was converted into a staff college for senior SS officers and was where they would complete their education. The commandant, SS-Obergruppenfuhrer Siegfried Taubert was formerly Heydrich's chief of staff and the father-in-law of Ernst Robert Grawitz, the SS medical chief.

The Centaur is a symbol of the dark and unruly forces of nature.

156

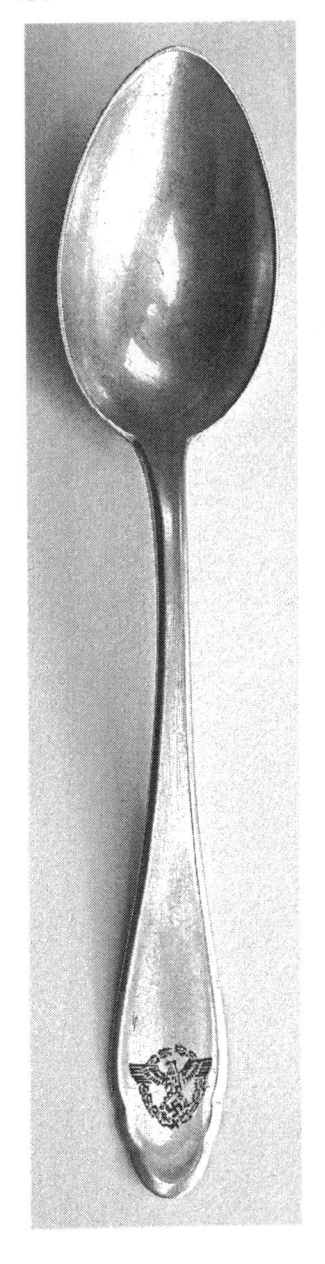

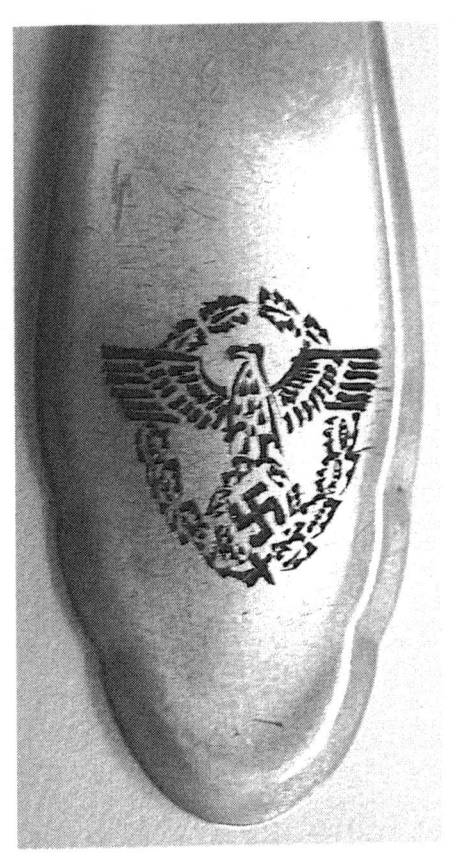

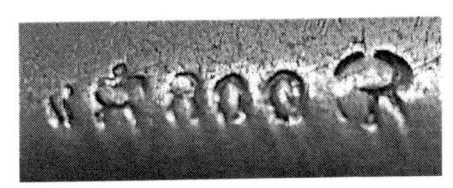

SS/P-69
L = 142 mm / 5 9/16"

SS/P-69 **Police**

Teaspoon. Obverse carries the Police eagle with the swastika which was added in 1933 while the reverse is maker marked: crescent, crown, '800' 'G' facing 'R'. for - Gebruder Reiner, Krumbach Bayern, founded 1914.

From Hitler's assumption of power in 1933 to 1936, his effort was to take unrestricted control of the police. In June 1936, Himmler was appointed as Chief of German Police - Chef der Deutsche Polizei. Himmler then merged the SS and the Police into a single 'State Protection Corps' or Staatsschutzkorps under Himmler as the Reichsfuhrer SS und Chef der Deutsche Polizei (RFSSuChdDP). To do this, he absorbed the police into the SS. The German Police now fell into two distinct groups: The Ordnungspolizei or Orpo, the uniformed police and the Sicherheitspolizei or Sipo, the security police. These two were folded into the RSHA - Reichssicherheitshauptamt (Reich Security Main Office) under Heydrich on 22 September 1939, just prior to the start of WWII. .

158

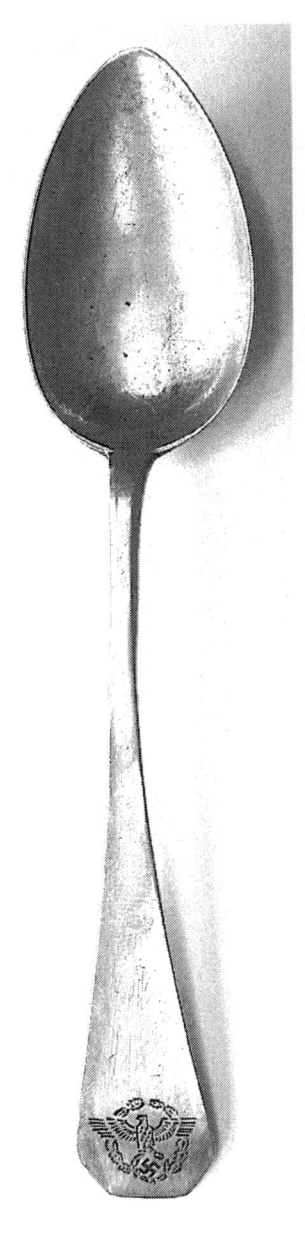

SS/P-70
L = 137 mm / 5 6/16"

SS/P-70 Police

Teaspoon. Obverse carries the police eagle with swastika. Reverse carries marker mark CB, 800 crescent moon and crown.

The police emblem is typically a six feathered eagle. The exception was sleeve eagles which were six feathered for NCO's and enlisted men whereas the Officers and Generals sleeve eagles were 3 feathered.

OrPo Ordnungspolizei although separate from the SS their commander was Oberst-Gruppenfuhrer Kurt Daluge. They maintained a system of insignia and ranks unique to OrPo. They were the uniformed, regular police force and as a result of their green uniform, they were called the grune polizei (green police).

SiPo Sicherheitspolizei or secret police included the gestapo (secret state police) and Kripo (criminal police) both under the SS.

It was Himmler's intent to wipe out the OrPo and have everyone under direct SS control.

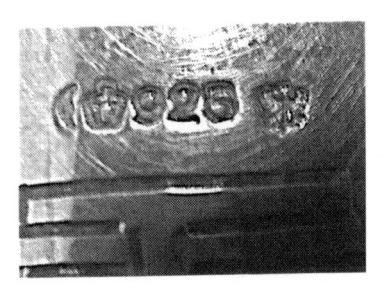

M-71

MISCELLANEOUS

M-71 HITLER Napkin Ring, (Serviettenring)

In Hitler's State Formal (Bruckmann) pattern. The upper and lower edges have a border in a Greek Key geometric "Meander" pattern attributed to Frau Professor Gerdy Troost. Hall marked with the Reichsmark composed of a crescent moon and a crown mark indicating silver made in Germany, followed by the silver content of 925 and then a spread eagle (Maker Mark of Bruckmann of Heilbronn). This one reportedly from the Obersalzberg residence near Bertesgaden in the Alps via a 101st Airborne veteran.

Maker marked: Nazi 'Fuhrer' Eagle and swastika with the initials AH on each side of the wreath held in the eagles talons. Stamped with "Bruckmann" followed by a crescent moon, a crown, "925" and an eagle. Measures: 1 3/4" H X 1 5/8" Diameter.

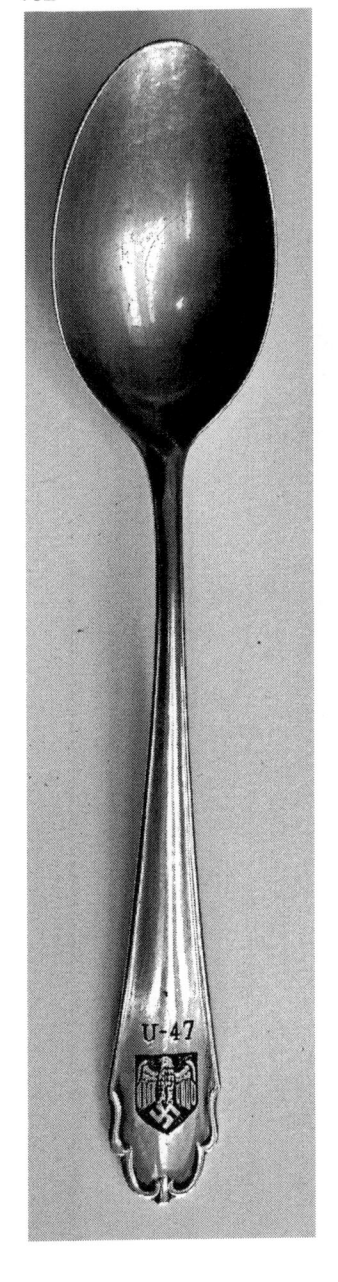

M-72
L = 160 mm / 6 5/16"

M-72 U-47

Commemorative teaspoon. Obverse carries U-47 over Eagle looking to his right. Reverse maker marked: Bruckmann, Reichmark, 800 and Bruckman's eagle.

The U-47, a 753-ton type VIIB submarine was built at Kiel, Germany and commissioned on 17 December 1938 with a crew of 53. On 13 October 1939, Cmdr. Gunther Prien set out in the U-47 in an attempt to attack the anchored British fleet harbored at Scapa Flow in the Orkney Islands. In a carefully planned operation, he made a daring penetration of the British anchorage and sank the battleship Royal Ark on the 14th of October 1939. Due to the poor reliability of German torpedos, he had to fire 8 torpedoes of which only 3 functioned properly. Prien became world famous, and resulted in he being the first Kriegsmariner awarded the Knight's Cross of the Iron Cross by Hitler personally on 18 October 1939. Prien and the U-47 continued their success and as the 4th highest scoring U-Boat ace credited with sinking 195,000 tons of allied shipping Prien was the 5th recipient of the Oak-leaves to the Knight's Cross of the Iron Cross on 20 Oct 1940. On 7 March 1941, while attacking a convoy south of Iceland, the U-47 was believed to have been sunk by the British destroyer Wolverine, killing Prien and his crew.

Trivia: The German rank of Ka-Leut (Kapitan Leutnant) was the rank assigned to U-Boat Captains. The Type VII submarine was the most produced type of war ship of all the navies in the world at 702.

164

Danziger Werft
Aktiengesellschaft

HANSA-ROSTFREI

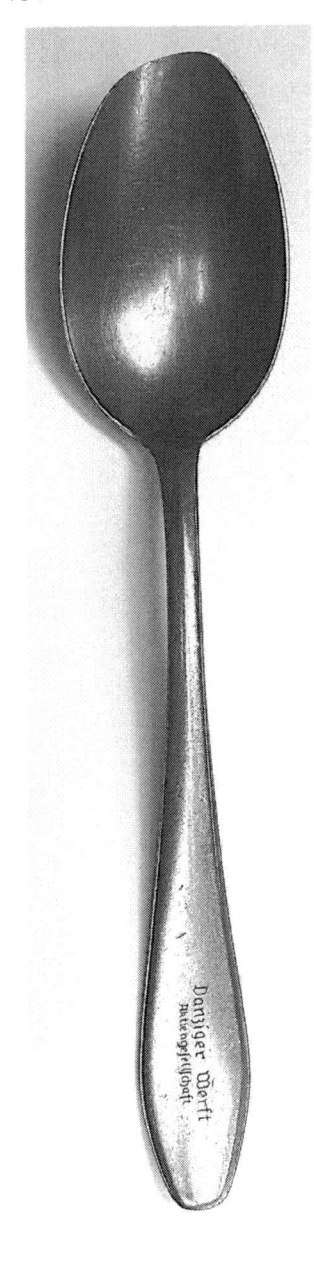

M - 73
L = 210- mm / 8 1/4"

M-73 Danziger Werft

Tablespoon. Obverse marked with Danziger Werft Aktiengesellschaft (Danzig Shipbuilding Corporation) which was opened in 1921 and closed in 1945. The spoon predates the 1933 mandatory use of the swastika. The reverse is marked 'Hansa-Rostfrei'

At the end of WWI, this shipyard was located in the Free State of Danzig instead of Poland due to the population being 80 percent German and was subsequently taken over by Germany in 1939. Located at the escape of the Vistula river to Gdansk Gulf, the yard delivered 42 Type VII U Boats to the Kriegsmarine between 16 December 1940 to 8 September 1943. When Danzig was taken over by the Polish government after WWII, the shipyard became the Gdansk Shipyard which gained international fame when Solidarity was founded there in 1980.

Trivia: During WWII, Germany commissioned a total of 1,174 U-boats, with 702 Type VII's and suffered the loss of 80 % of their submarine crews totaling 28,751 men lost.

166

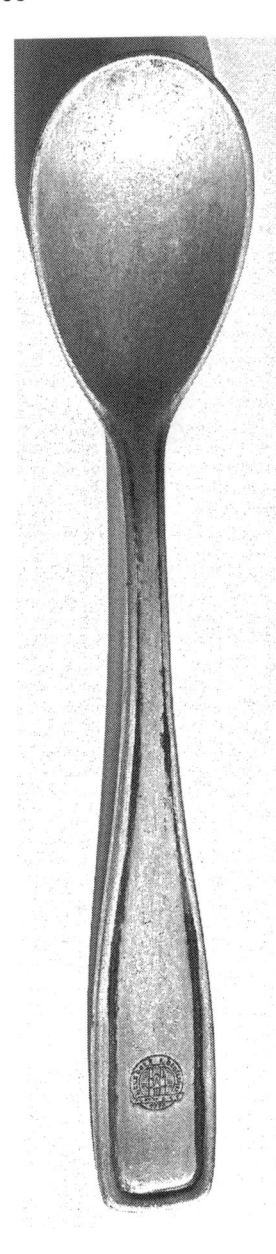

M-74
L = 139 mm / 5 7/16"

M-74 Haus der Deutschen Arbeit

Sugar spoon This is a very rare spoon with HdD Ar. insignia impressed on the obverse and dated 1933. On the reverse, the Wellner name and maker mark (a die in a circle, showing the 4 side) and "90" in a circle, "16" in a square.

Shortly after Hitler assumed power, he banned trade unions on 2 May 1933. Per James Pool's Hitler and His Secret Partners, eighty-nine union leaders were arrested and total union assets of 184,000,000 marks were seized - enough money to support the Nazi party for over a year. On 10 May 1933, the Deutsche Arbeitsfront (DAF) was formed by the incorporation of all formerly free and independent trade unions. Haus der Deutschen Arbeit may have been one of those free and independent trade union houses that was disbanded by the SA and "co-ordinated" by Robert Ley into the DAF during May 1933.

A second possibility is that the HdD Ar was actually a union hall, possibly on the national level, and not itself a union per se as a literal translation is 'National Labor Hall'.

Note: Special group silverware is extremely hard to find, especially for the smaller more exotic groups of this period.

M - 75

M-75 OFFICER'S FIELD BESTECK

This matched set of a knife, fork and spoon is from J. A. Henckels and was used by German Army officers when in the field. The knife is maker marked with the Henkels trademarked 'two stick figures' and impressed with "J.A.Henckels" over "SOLINGEN". When folded, the three pieces fit into a companion buckskin lined leather pouch that snaps shut.

Spoon folded: 112 mm / 4 6/16"
Spoon open: 198 mm / 7 3/4"

M-76

M-76 Army Field Issue Folding Spoon / Fork Combination Cutlery Set (Essbesteck)

This is the standard issue, aluminum construction folding tablespoon and four tine fork combination. On the reverse of the spoon handle is an embossed, unidentified manufacturers initials (WSuCL) in a rectangular border. Owners initials, "LB" scratched on the front of the fork between the arrow and the pivotal rivet .

Folded length is 6 inches while opened length is 9 1/2 inches.

M-77
L = 209 mm / 8 1/4"

M -77 VEB Wellner - Post Script

Wellner survived the war and as a result of being located in eastern Germany, became VEB Wellner (Volkseigener Betrieb - People-owned Enterprise) or state owned workplace of the German Democratic Republic / Deutsche Demokratische Republik which existed from 1949 to 1990. Today the closed facility is: Wellner Silber GmbH at Wellner Str 61,, Aue, Germany. having not survived the German reunification.

The soup spoon is marked "VEB v. Wellner - 90 (in circle) - 45 (in a square).

The author visits the abandoned Wellner complex.

M-78
L = 128 mm / 5 1/16"

M-78 Bayerischer Hof Hotel, Munick

Sugar Spoon. From the (no swastika), period of struggle 1921-1933. Maker marked with a stick figure of a man walking with a walking stick followed by BMF 30

Luxury hotels that were favored by Hitler, particularly in the earliest years, the years of struggle - Der Kampfzeit - the struggle for power - the period prior to 1933, were the Hotel Dreesen, Bad Godesberg, Hotel Kaiserhof, Berlin, Hotel Bayerischer Hof, Munick and for Nazi Party Days, Der Deutsche Hof, Nuremberg and after the war started, the Hotel Casino, Zoppot/Sopot, N. Poland / Baltic Sea / Danzig was used as his HQ for Polish Campaign of 19-25 September 1939. After the mandatory requirement for the use of the Nazi swastika, some of the hotels saved the expense of new service utensils by such clever solutions as attaching the swastika to the outside bottom of the tea and coffee pots.

Hitler had a weakness for luxury in automobiles too. A Mercedes Benz advertisement showed Hitler about to board an enormous Benz with the headline, "Hitler leaves Landsberg Prison." Much later he had even the more enormous 6 wheeled Mercedes: The Black one was registered to the NSDAP while the Gray one (used for his triumphal entry into Austria during the Anschluss) was registered to the Liebstandarte-SS.

M-79
L = 112 mm / 4 7/16"

M-79 Martin Bormann vs Nurnburg Rally Souvenir

Martin Bormann: Dealer states: "the Martin Bormann egg spoon came directly from Bormann's house wreckage at the Obersalzberg! a very rare and extremely difficult to locate pattern from Martin Bormann." (Born 1900) - Head of the Party Chancellery and private secretary of the Fuhrer, who by the end of WWII had become second only to Hitler in terms of real political power and an SS general!

vs

A typical souvenir (Andenkens) offered at the prewar, annual NSDAP rallies (Reichsparteitag) held in early September and focused on strengthening Hitler's position as Germany's savior. Each year had a rally theme:

   1933 Rally of Victory
      (Hitler to Power)
   1938 Rally of Greater Germany
      (Austria annexed)

Obverse: Eagle looking to his left, 'Reverse: marked "Aluminium-Germany" with a handcrafted symbol of Nurenburg in the center of the words.'

Problems!

Would Martin Bormann, Hitler's private secretary, use an aluminum spoon to eat his soft boiled egg in the morning?

and

The "handcrafted symbol of Nuremberg" has the stripes slanting down to the left whereas the actual city symbol has the stripes slanting down to the right.

Your comments are solicited in this matter

Material and Length Listing

PS-1 Adolf Hitler, Formal Pattern	800	146 mm
PS-2 Adolf Hitler, Curved 'AH',	800	148 mm
PS-3 Adolf Hitler, Ornamental	90	139 mm
PS-4 Adolf Hitler, Raised ribs	Alpacca	134 mm
PS-5 Eva Braun, Baroque with EB Butterfly	46?	142 mm
PS-6 Eva Braun, Parfait Spoon	90	212 mm
PS-7 Herman Goering, Coat of Arms	800	137 mm
PS-8 Herman Goering, Reichsmarshall	800	145 mm
PS-9 Heinrich Himmler, Train Pattern	90	141 mm
PS-10 Heinrich Himmler, Script Monogram	?	138 mm
PS-11 Albert Speer, Intertwined Block AS	60	140 mm
PS-12 Helmut Weidling, Personal Pattern	90	143 mm
PS-13 Bernard Rust, Deutsche-Hochschule, DH	90	210 mm

PS-14 Bernard Rust, Deutsche-Hochschule, DH	90	109 mm
PS-15 Dr. Robert Ley, Deutsche Arbeitsfront, DAF	90	216 mm
PS-16 Ernst Kaltenbrunner, Ornamental EK (Ice Tea)	100	224 mm
PS-17 Fritz Sauckel, Thuringian Eagle with broken wing pattern	90	213 mm
PS-18 Hans Frank, Governor General of Poland	90	217 mm
OG-19 NSDAP-Fraktur	800	133 mm
OG-20 NSDAP High Leader Swastika with Oak Leaves	800	141 mm
OG-21 NSDAP / SA Early Version	Al	211 mm
OG-22 SA Sturmabteilung (Stormtrooper)	800	145 mm
OG-23 SA Sturmabteilung	800	143 mm
OG-24 HJ Hitler-Jugend (Hitler Youth)	800	132 mm
OG-25 HJ - RFS / (Leadership School)	90	213 mm
OG-26 National Labor Service RAD - Reichs Arbeitsdienst 1936	RF	217 mm

OG-27 German National Railways 800　140 mm
　　　DR-Deutsche Reichsbahn,
　　　AH 205

OG-28 German National Railways 800　211 mm
　　　DR - AH 205

OG-29 German National Railways 90　216 mm
　　　DR - Goering 243

OG-30 Reich Chancellery RK -　800　210 mm
　　　Neu Reichskanzlei, Berlin

OG-31 Deutsche Rotes Kreuz　800　136 mm

OG-32 RLB, Air Raid Protection　800　142 mm

OG-33 Student Federation　800　149 mm

OG-34 Eagle facing right　RF　141 mm
　　　over 1942

W-35 Army Mess, Deutsche Heer,　AL　212 mm
　　　W.S.M.42

W-36 Army Mess, Wehrmacht Heer　AL　210 mm
　　　"WH" Armed Forces Army

W-37 Army Mess, Aluminum　AL　209 mm
　　　'LGK&F 39

W-38 Army Mess, Aluminum　AL　139 mm
　　　B.A. F. N. 39

W-39 Army Commemorative?　800　142 mm
　　　1944 over Eagle over D.H.

W-40 Army, H.U. - Quarters		Pot	153 mm
W-41 Africa Corps D.AK Deutsches Afrika Korps		800	145 mm
W-42 Africa Corps D-AK		800	144 mm
W-43 Navy Mess, HHL Rustfrei		RF	212 mm
W-44 Navy Mess, Blancadur		AL	144 mm
W-45 Air Force Mess, Droop Tail Luftwaffe Eagle		RF	206 mm
W-46 Air Force Mess, Oxydex		RF	210 mm
W-47 Air Force Officer's Service		plate	209 mm
W-48 Air Force General Officer's Service		90	207 mm
W-49 Air Force Officer's Service		90	142 mm
W-50 Air Force General Officers Service with "B" monogram		800	174 mm
SS-51 LSSAH, 1st SS-Lieberstandarte		90	208 mm
SS-52 LSSAH, Becker		90	144 mm
SS-53 LSSAH, "1941", WMF		800	138 mm
SS-54 LSSAH, LW		800	136 mm
SS-55 2nd SS-Pz Div, Reich "XX"		800	140 mm

SS-56	SS-Reich, LSF	800	139 mm
SS-57	SS-Reich, (Lightening)	Alpacca	146 mm
SS-58	SS-Reich, Textured SS	?	138 mm
SS-59	3rd SS-Panzer Division SS-Death's-Head Div,	800	141 mm
SS-60	5th SS-Panzer Division SS-Div. 'Wiking'	RF	215 mm
SS-61	9th SS Panzer Division SS-Div Hohenstaufen	800	133 mm
SS-62	11th SS-Freiwilligen- Pz-Grenadier Div'Nordland '	800	145 mm
SS-63	Waffen SS	Alpacca	149 mm
SS-64	SS, P100, Raised SS	P100	133 mm
SS-65	SS, SS in a double circle,	800	142 mm
SS-66	SS - Ornate Mocka spoon crossed hammers & E. Kludas	800	127 mm
SS-67	SS-Wewelsburg, Commander's Service	800	216 mm
SS-68	SS-Wewelsburg, Leaders School	20	211 mm
SS-69	SS/P- Police	800	142 mm
SS-70	SS/P - Police	800	137 mm

M-71 Adolf Hitler Napkin Ring,	925	43 mm
M-72 U-47 Commemorative,	800	160 mm
M-73 Danziger Werft	RF	210 mm
M-74 Haus der Deutschen Arbeit,	90	139 mm
M-75 Officer's Field Service	RF	
M-76 Wehrmacht Fieldgear	AL	
M-77 Wellner of East German	90	209 mm
M-78 Bayerischer Hof Hotel	30	128 mm
M-79 Bormann vs Nurnburg	AL	112 mm
AD-80 Waffen-SS	800	208 mm
AD-81 Kriegsmarine	RF	211 mm
AD-82 NSKOV	800	217 mm
AD-83 HJ Sportsschule, Braunau	90	212 mm
AD-84 Heer JRS 41	RF	202 mm
AD-85 Deutsche Reichsbahn	800	142 mm
AD-86 SS Neusilber	NS	211 mm
AD-87 K.L. Buchenwald	RF	139 mm
AD-88 Deutsche Christen	800	218 mm

To transpose mm to inches, multiply by 0.0394. Thus 210mm X 0.0394 = approximately 8 1/4 inches.

German decimal silver standard marks: .800 and .925 attest to the purity of the silver as 80% and 92.5% with the remainder copper.

Silver plated German cutlery: Per a contemporary Wellner input, silver plating is only done using pure silver. If the normal maker mark is followed by a '90' it indicates that 90 grams (3.2 oz) of silver is applied per a surface area of 24 qdm (quadradezimeter), equivalent to 24 cutlery pieces (6 each: teaspoons, tablespoons, knives and forks). The second number (100, 60, 46, 20 etc,) require more research and remains a mystery to me. A second cut from WMF: 90g plate is 90 grams of silver on 24 square decimeters = 372 sqin on the corresponding surface of 24 menu spoons.

Herstellungszeichen or Makers Mark

The German Silver Makers Guild mandated that at least part of all cutlery sets carry the silver designation. This explains why some pieces of broken sets turn up with no designation.

Tomback is an alloy of copper and zinc. Replaced during the late war with pure zinc

Cupal: Aluminum between two thin sheets of copper.
Usually surface plated with silver or gilt.

Leichtmetall or Lightweight alloy

Kriegsmetall or War Metal was a poor quality alloy of zinc, copper and lead. Commonly called 'Pot Metal' by collectors.

Biliography

Angolia, John R. and Schlicht, Adolf, Uniforms & Traditions of the German Army 1933 - 1945, Bender Publishing, Second Printing November 1992 in 3 volumes.

Buchner, Alex, The German Infantry Handbook 1939 - 1945, Schiffr Military History, 1991

Cameron, Norman and Stevens, R. H., translators, Hitler's Table Talk, Enigma Books 1988

Coates, E.J., The U-Boat Commanders Handbook, Thomas Publications, 1989

Griffith, Mark D., "Liberated" Adolf Hitler Memorabilia, Ulric of England, 1986

Haddock, Chase with Snyder, Charles E., Treasure Trove, The Looting of the Third Reich.

Hamilton, Charles, Leader's & Personalities of the Third Reich Volume 1, 2nd Edition Bender Publishing 1996

Hamilton, Charles, Leader's & Personalities of the Third Reich Volume 2, First Edition Bender Publishing 1996

Johnson, Aaron L., Hitler's Military Headquarters, Bender Publishing, 1999

Johnson, Paul Louis, Horses of the German Army in World War II. Schigger Military History, 2006

Keegab, John, Waffen SS, Ballentine Books, 1970

Lumsden, Robin, The Allgemeine-SS, Osprey Publishing, 2004

Lumsden, Robin, Himmler's Black Order 1923-45. Sutton Publishing, 1997

McCombs, Don & Worth, Fred World War II, 4,139 Strange and Fascinating Facts. Wings Books, 1983

MacLean, French L. 2000 Quotes From Hitler's 1000-Year Reich, Schiffer, 2007

Pool, James Who Financed Hitler 1919 - 1933, Pocket Books 1997

Pool, James, Hitler and His Secret Partners, 1933-1945. Pocket Books, 1997

Speer, Albert. Inside the Third Reich, Avon Books 1970

Toland, John, Hitler, The Pictorial Documentary of His Life, Doubleday, 1978

Windrow, Martin, The Waffen-SS, Osprey Publishing, 2004

Wistrich, Robert, Who's Who in Nazi Germany, Bonanza Books, 1982

The internet is a great help for research

Historical Addendum

Population comparison - 1939

Greater Germany	69 million
Russia	169 million
USA	131 million
UK	48 million

German Military Philosophy

German military success was to be based on superior leadership, organization, supply and morale. This was believed to overcome material / manpower limitations. In War and Peace, Leo Tolstoy observed that the effectiveness of an army is "the product of a mass multiplied by something else; by an unknown X...the spirit of the army." A more realistic assessment made when Germany invaded Russia: "the German's came to play tennis, the game was actually rugby".

Military Reality

In 1933 Germany had a 100,000 man Military as prescribed by the Treaty of Versailles in 1920. The Wehrmacht was founded on 15Mar35 and the German military was expanded to 3,343,000 in 5 years under Hitler. Wehrmacht: 1Sep39 = 3,180,000, (with 2.7M heer). Under the reintroduction of conscription in 1935, each service allotment of available recruits was: Heer 66%, Luftwaffe 25% and Kriegsmarine 9%. Actually, the Heer typically made up 75% of the Wehrmacht and within the Heer, 82% were Infantry Divisions. The Wehrmacht maxed at 9.5M (5.5M Heer) and on 9May45 still had 7.8 Million under arms with 5.3 million in the Heer).

As early as 9 November 1939, the German Army shortened their marching boots by 3 to 5 cm (1 to 2 inches) to save leather which was already in short supply. While production of the Army Officer's leather greatcoat was not prohibited until 29 February 1944.

Volkssturm's "people's army" (formed in 1944) of 6 million old men and boys armed with the true Volksgewehr / (peoples rifle)- the Italian Carcano rifle, confiscated from Italy when Italy withdrew from the war. in 1943.

German Military Served and KIA + MIA

	Served	KIA & MIA	%
Heer / Army	13.6 M	4.2 M	31
Luftwaffe	2.5 M	,433M	17.3
Kriegsmarine	1.2 M	. 138M	11.5
W-SS	.9 M	.314M	34.9

The War in the East

In 1941, prior to the June invasion of Russia: Germany had 3,500 tanks and German Intelligence estimated Russian tanks at 10,000.   Russia actually had 24,000.
German Air Intelligence estimated Russian A/C at 10,500.
       Russia actually had 18,000.
German Foreign Armies East estimated Red Army at 2 Million, with war level of 4M. Actual was 4.2 Million. By invasion day, 5 Million.
In the 51st day of the invasion, Gen. Halder said that German intelligence originally estimated Russian Forces at 200 divisions and so far had identified 360!

Germany's surprise attack on The Soviet Union started on 22 June 1941 with 3.2 Million soldiers, 2,000 aircraft, 3,350 tanks, 7,184 pieces of artillery and 750,000 horses. In 10 days they had advanced 350 miles, started the Leningrad siege on 8 Sept. 41 took Minsk in August and Kiev in Sept, reached Moscow suburbs in December. By the end of 1941, almost 1 Million Soviet jews had been murdered, all before the "Final Solution" Wannsee Conference of Jan 42.

From the invasion of Russia (Operation Barbarosa) on 22 June 41 to 8 May 45, German Losses in the East were 1,015,000 dead, 4 Million wounded and 1.3 Million missing-in-action while the Red Army suffered 14 Million casualties with over 10 Million dead. The initial casualty rate was 16 Russians for every German. In 1941, German forces took 3.5 Million Russian POW's of a ultimate total of 5 Million, only 1.5 Million survived the war. Over 400,000 Russian died in the Battle for Berlin. Total estimated Russian civilian/ military killed in the East, 30 Million.

Prior to 1943, the standard German infantry division contained some 900 assorted gasoline powered vehicles consuming an average of 20 tons of fuel daily as well as 5,300+ horses consuming 58 tons of fodder daily.

Hitler

Versailles Treaty of 1919 - repudiated by Hitler. In 1935, Hitler renewed conscription, founded the Luftwaffe and started submarine production in June, 1936 renewed arms production, and remilitarized the Rhineland (Mar), annexed Austria Mar 1938, annexed Sudetenland 30 Sep 38, Annexed Czechoslovakia 15 Mar 39 and finally declared war on Poland 1 Sep 39.

In Sept 1938, as a result of the "Munich Agreement" between Britain, France and Germany, the North Eastern Czechoslovakian Sudetenland was ceded to Germany, allegedly as Hitler's last territorial claim in Europe. On 14 March 1939 the German army marched into what remained of Czechoslovakia, unopposed and established the German Protectorate of Bohemia & Moravia and the independent state of Slovakia which in reality was just a puppet state of the Germans.

Per Hitler: "All administration of justice is a political activity. Time honored commentaries have become wastepaper, the "creative personality' of the National Socialist judge was liberated from the mortmain of the past. The whole body of previous interpretations of the statutes laboriously built up by German Jurists, no longer constituted precedents of value."

NAZI music: Hitler was equated to Wagner's hero Siegfried. Franz Liszt's 'Les Preludes' was always used to accompany film footage of dive bombers and also was the signature theme for the 'Sondermeldung' or "special announcements" that periodically interrupted normal radio programming to announce victories. In 1940-42, "We're Marching Against England" was the big hit. In 1944 "Dancing Together Into Heaven" was banned due to the success of allied bombing. Mozart's 'Requiem' banned as too depressing. "Fidelio' and 'William Tell' banned due to their themes of liberty triumphing over tyranny. Per Albert Speer's book 'Inside the Third Reich', he quotes Hitler, " You'll hear that (Liszt's Les Preludes) often in the near future, because it is going to be our victory fanfare for the Russian Campaign". "For each of the previous campaigns Hitler had personaly chosen a musical fanfare that preceded radio announcements of striking victories."

Hitler's yacht: Built by the Blohm & Voss shipyard of Hamburg and originally launched on 15 Dec 1934 as the Versuchboot Grille (Training Boat-Cricket), in 1935 it was re-designated as the "Aviso Grille". (Dispatch or advice/

intelligence boat-Cricket), and became Adolf Hitler's personal state yacht harbored at Kiel. It had an overall length of 443 feet making it the largest yacht afloat. It had three, 22.7cm cannon, 6 antiaircraft guns and 2 or 3 machine guns and a capacity of carrying 280 mines. Hitler being, "landsinning", (land-minded), and subject to seasickness, only boarded the Aviso Grille on a few occasions and shortly after the outbreak of WWII the Aviso Grille was utilized as an auxiliary mine sweeper in the Baltic and North seas. In the autumn of 1942 the Aviso Grille was posted to Norway as a floating Staff Headquarters for the German U-boat commander stationed in Narvik. Confiscated by the British at the end of the war the Aviso Grille was eventually privately purchased and used as a cruise ship in the Mediterranean for a period of time until it was finally scrapped in the USA in 1951. As noted by Army General of Infantry Gunther Blumentritt, "Only the admirals had a happy time in this war - as Hitler knew nothing about the sea, whereas he felt he knew about land warfare."

Bandenweiler Marsch: Adolf Hitler's very own personal march played by his SS band, ONLY when Hitler was in the immediate vicinity. His 'Hail to the Chief'.

Hitler's 6 wheeled Mercedes: The Black one was registered to the NSDAP while the Gray one (used for his triumphal entry into Austria during the Anschluss) was registered to the Liebstandarte-SS.

Although born a Catholic, Hitler despised religion as a crutch for the weak and believed that the idea of Christian equality protected the racially inferior of the world. (Germany was 1/3 catholic and 2/3 rds Protestant.) Hitler privately declared that one could not be German and a Christian! Per famed psychologist Carl Jung...the decent and well-meaning German people are "intelligent enough not only to believe

but to know that the God of the Germans is Wotan and not the Christian God."
Regarding the Treaty of Versailles: In 1922, Hitler said, "We do not pardon, we demand vengeance."

To manufacture the Volkswagon, Hitler had the town of Wolfsburg created. (None were ever delivered!) His nick name was Wolf, his sister was forced to change her name to "Wolf"!

Der Kampfzeit = the struggle for power

Regarding his opposition: "Achievements which appear to strengthen the country do but increase their hatred. They are in permanent opposition. They are not filled with a desire to help the people, but rather by a hope which severs them from the people - the hope that the government may fail in its work for the people. They are for that reason never prepared to admit the benefit resulting from any act; rather they are filled with the determination to deny on principle every success and on every success to trace the failures and the weaknesses which may possibly ensue" AH 13 July 1934 Reichstag.

As Hitler was the Reichskanzler, actually he was Germany's 23rd Chancellor, he had a Reichskanzlei at Bischofweisen, Bavaria starting in 1937 and the Neureichskanzlei or New Chancellery in Berlin designed and built by Albert Speer in 1939 at a today's estimated cost of $ 1 billion!

Nazi Swastika / Flags

The Swastika is a sanskrit word meaning "well being" and is an ancient symbol used by many cultures signifying the cycle of life as well as the sun. It was also a Nordic rune and the pagan Germanic symbol for Thor, God of

Adventurers. During WWI the swastika began to represent national and anti-semetic leanings in such organizations as the Thule society and other German nationalistic movements and later, assorted Freikorps groups. In the midsummer of 1920, Hitler adopted the swastika as the premier symbol of the NSDAP and takes credit for the swastika's final presentation in red, black and white in Mein Kampf.

From Wikipedia: Nazi Flags: The Nazi party used a right-facing swastika as their symbol and the red and black colors were said to represent Blut und Boden (blood and soil). Black, white, and red were in fact the colors of the old North German Confederation flag (invented by Otto von Bismarck, based on the Prussian colors black and white). In 1871, with the foundation of the German Reich, the flag of the North German Confederation became the German Reichsflagge (Reich's flag). Black, white, and red became the colors of the nationalists through the following history (for example World War I and the Weimar Republic).

Neutrals

War is dependent on money. To quote Cicero, 106-43 B.C. "Endless money forms the sinews of war." Germany spent an estimated $ 80 billion on their military buildup between 1933 and 1939. Some 170 Infantry Divisions were created during this period. let alone an air force. Since Germany was close to bankruptcy in 1939, the money 'Gold' was taken from the defeated countries. Nazi procedure was to offer conquered countries German currency in exchange for the countries gold reserves. Belgium refused and Germany simply confiscated their gold. This helped other countries to opt for exchange. The total gold from conquered countries was in the 100's of millions if not billions of dollars in monetary gold which was converted into war material from "neutral" countries. The five European countries that remained neutral during WWII were Ireland, Portugal, Spain, Sweden and Switzerland. Their contributions to the German war effort included: Viche France (trucks), Switzerland (tools & ball bearings), Sweden (steel, iron ore & ball bearings), Rumania (oil), Spain (leather goods), Portugal (food), Turkey (tobacco and chromium, being essentially the sole supplier to NAZI Germany of this key industrial metal. By 1943, Germany had only 6 months supply of chromium). Without supplies from "neutrals", Germany could not have waged war beyond 1943! In addition, German coal paid for the problem free movement of German military equipment from Germany to Italy via the Swiss road and rail system. In 1942, Himmler stated, "The Swedes are parasites who have reaped the profits from two wars."

Nuremberg / Nurnberg War Crimes Trials

On 1 October 1946, death sentences were passed down at the Nuremberg trials for twelve of the 24 Nazi leaders tried. Goring had committed suicide on the 15th and Martin Bormann was in absentia. The remaining 10 were executed on 16 October 1946 in the following order: 1. Joachim von Ribbentrop, Nazi Minister of Foreign Affairs 1938-1945, 2. Field Marshal Wilhelm Keitel, Head of OKW 1938-1945, 3. Ernst Kaltenbrunner, Highest surviving SS leader of RSHA 1943-1945 Central Nazi Intelligence Organ, 4. Alfred Rosenberg, Minister of Eastern Occupied Territories, 5. Hans Frank, Reich Law Leader 1935-1945 and Governor General of Poland 1939-1945, 6. Wilhelm Frick, Minister of Interior 1933-1943 and Reich Protector of Bohemia-Moravia 1943-1945, 7. Julius Streicher, Gauleiter of Franconia 1922-1945 and publisher of "Der Sturmer", 8. Fritz Sauckel, Gauleiter of Thuringia 1927-1945 and Plenipotentiary of the Nazi slave labor program 1942-1945. 9. Colonel-General

Alfred Jodl, 10, Arthur Seyss-Inquart, Reich Commissioner of the Occupied Netherlands 1940-1945

> Trivia: Field Marshall Keitel was the first professional soldier to be executed under the "new concept" of International law where by soldiers could no longer claim exemption due to "dutifully carrying out superior's orders".

As an aside, my wife and I visit Germany every Spring, during white asparagus time. Having visited any number of antique shops in Germany, I can truthfully say that is no shortage of 3rd Reich period silverware and at very reasonable prices. To set up a small engraving operation to turn out 3rd Reich logo'd silverware would be a piece of cake except that the German authorities are quite against it. Unfortunately the same can not be said for Austria.

Comment on Hitler's Formal Service

Sets of Hitler's "formal" tableware were distributed to 6 locations. Each locations set size was believed to serve a maximum of 20 to 25 people. The cutlery (bestecke) flatware pieces known to me manufactured by Bruckmann include:

dinner spoon,	dinner fork	dinner knife
luncheon spoon,	luncheon fork	luncheon knife
demitasse spoon	demitasse fork	demitasse knife
ice cream spoon	desert fork	fruit knife
ice tea spoon	fish fork	fish knife
lemon press	oyster fork,	napkin ring

Complimented by serving items such as: asparagus server, aspic server, pie server, sauce ladle, salad serving fork and spoon, gravy ladle, meat fork, serving spoon. pickle fork, butter knife, salt & pepper shakers. In addition from Wellner came serving vessels, coffee pots, tea pots, sugar bowls, creamers, casserole dish, roaster dish, gravy boat, bread plate, serving tray, warming plate, coasters, various sized serving trays. As an example, the 20 to 25 place settings at each location would typically have 6 serving vessels for such things as vegetables, mashed potatoes, stew etc. or the "Eintopf" or one-serving, compulsory meal served during the war years and therefore would need 6 serving spoons at each location for a total of 36 pieces which incidentally, were 10 inches long with a 2 inch wide bowl.

The mathematics are interesting! Bruckmann gifted 3,000 pieces of the formal ware to Hitler on his 50th birthday, 20 April 1939. Assuming each of the six locations received approximately 500 items and if a place setting could require a minimum of 18 different table items, as identified above, and with 25 place settings at each of the 6 locations equals 150 settings times 18 cutlery items equals 2,700 pieces of cutlery and 300 other items. Any additional cutlery items would add 150 to the cutlery total while reducing the servings total accordingly. This also suggests that Hitler's use of his formal tableware was limited to relatively small, intimate groups and that the meals were 'family style'. My own observation is that from anecdotal comments and common sense, between lost, damaged and as Hitler's private silver ware was in high demand as souvenirs during his life, attrition must have led to orders for replacements which indicates that the 3,000 quantity was the base number for this service.

Special Wellner mystery,

My wife and I visited the Wellner factory in Aue, Germany during the spring of 2008. Unfortunately, we made the trip on a sunday. Actually the day was of little consequence as the factory complex has been closed and abandoned. I have been in contact with a Wellner employee and is as mystified as I am by the markings Wellner uses. Inquiries to Aue drew helpful responses from not only the mayor but also the City museum. Complete clarification remains underway.

Spoon		
PS-11	60	??
PS-12	90	21
PS-15	90	45
PS-16	100	24
M - 67	90	16

What does the 21, 45, 24, 16 represent???

WELLNER
90

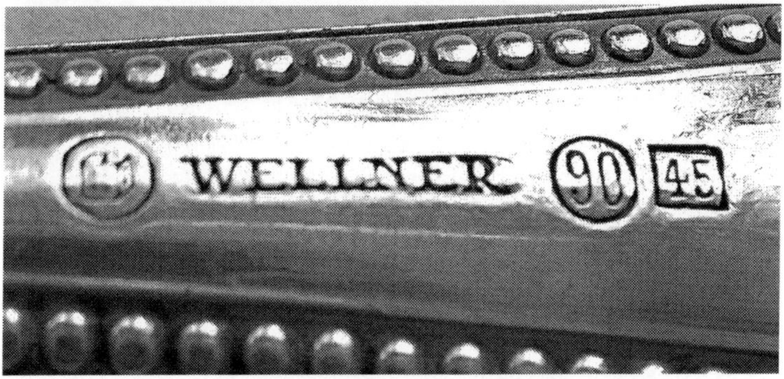
WELLNER
90
45

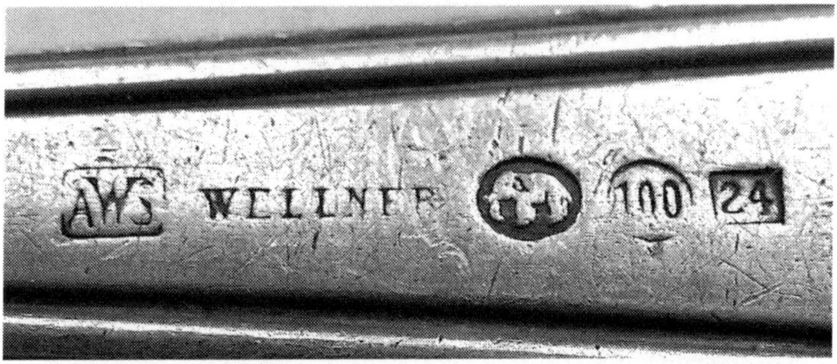
AWS
100
24

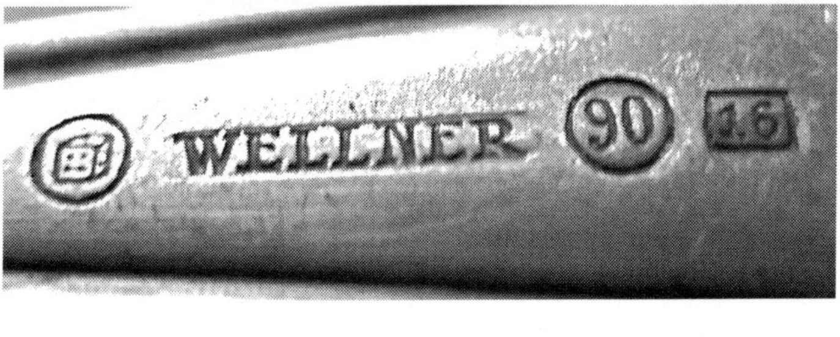
WELLNER
90

ADDENDUM

AD-80 Waffen-SS tablespoon

AD-81 Kriegsmarine Tablespoon, no 'M'

AD-82 NSKOV

AD-83 HJ Sportsschule Braunau

AD-84 Heer, A.W.JRS 41

AD-85 Deutsche Reichsbahn - DR

AD-86 SS, neusilber

AD-87 K.L. Buchenwald

AD-88 Deutsche Christen - DC

Things too Interesting to Leave Out

Comment and Corrections

And Finally

Fini

200

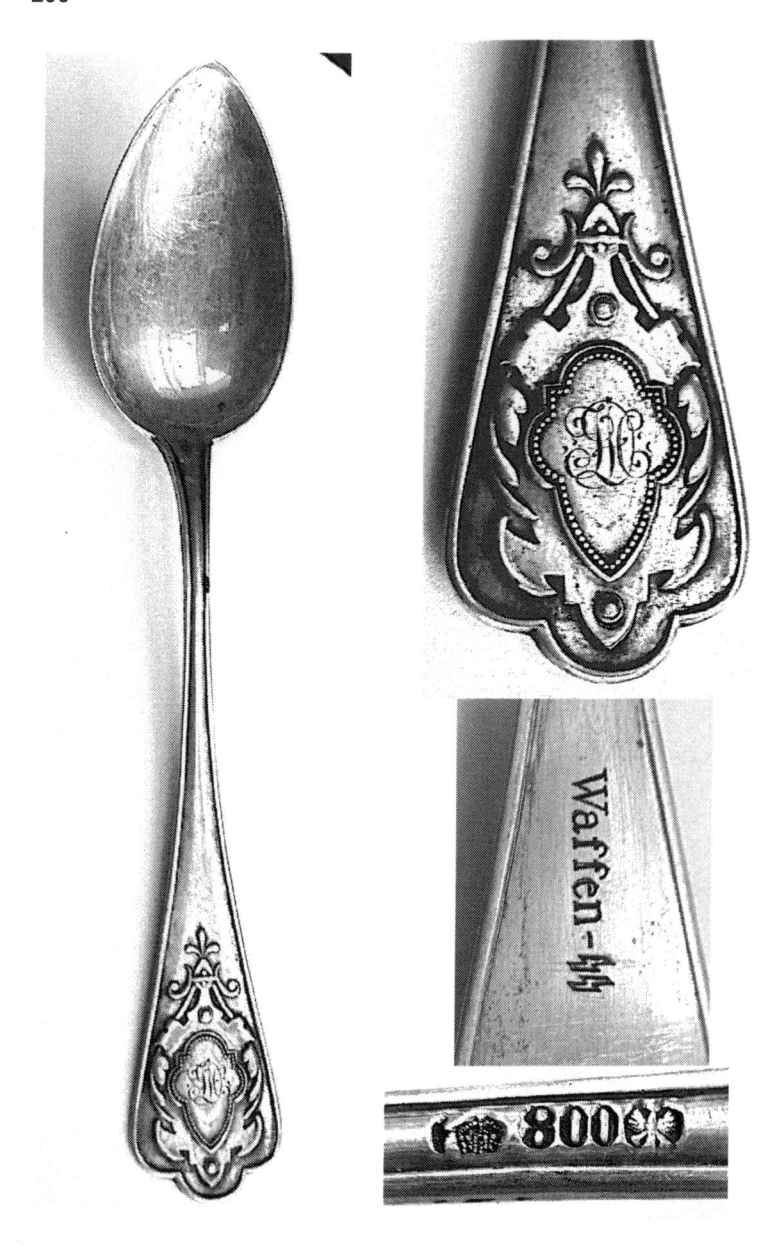

AD-80 Waffen-SS

Tablespoon, Obverse baroque with engraved owner initials of 'DJC'. Reverse with impressed 'Waffen-SS', and crescent moon. crown, 800 and a Bruckmann & Sohne trade mark 'eagle'.

On 26 July 1934, Adolf Hitler announced that "in consideration of the very meritorious service of the SS, especially in connection with the events of 30th June 1934,(night of the Long Knives when the SA leadership was killed) I elevate it to the status of an independent organization within the National Socialist Worker's Party."

Originally, Waffen-SS personnel requirements called for a minimum height of 5'11" for all volunteers except for the LAH which required a minimum height of 6'1".

The term 'Waffen-SS' was made official during Feb 1940.

Special note; Although Austria had only 8 percent of the population of Germany, it supplied 14 percent of the SS manpower.

208 mm / 8 3/16"

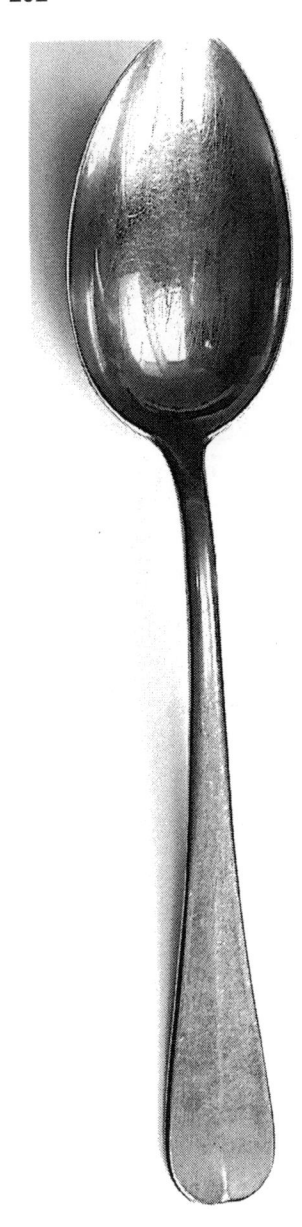

AD-81
211 mm / 8 5/16"

AD-81 Kriegsmarine

Tablespoon Kreigsmarine. Obverse of the handle is unmarked with a low, central ridge. Reverse marker marked F.W.W. 41. Impressed Kreigsmarine eagle with 3 feathers but no 'M', Rustfrei.

"The U-Boat Commander's Handbook, New Edition 1943" was translated by the US Navy and published by Thomas Publications in 1989. This handbook was the bible for the 1,244 German naval officers that served as U-Boat commanders.

The U-Boat pens at Lorient, France used 250,000 tons of cement and 17,000 tons of steel and are still in use by the French navy.

On 4 May 1945 - Messages were sent to all U-Boats to cease action. On 5 May, the U-835 sank a collier four miles off Point Judith, Rhode Island and in turn was the last German U-boat sunk with the loss of all hands.

204

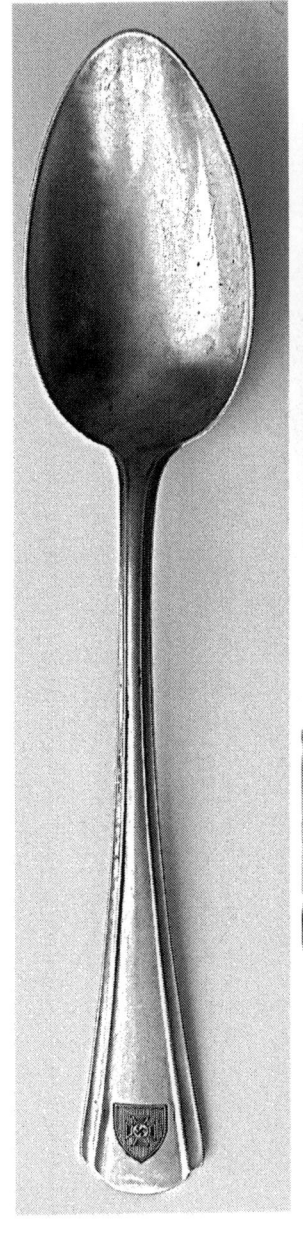

AD-82
217 mm / 8 9/16"

AD-82   NS-Kriegsopferversorgung

Soupspoon: The obverse carries the NSKOV shield composed of a black mobile swastika within a circle and the circle set against a black iron cross all within a shield. The reverse carries the maker mark of Koch & Bergfeld, Bremen, founded 1829, 800, crescent and crown.

The NSKOV (National Socialist War Victim's Welfare Service or War Disabled Support Organization)) was established in 1930 and institutionalized in 1935 as a social welfare organization to assist NSDAP party members who had become disabled as a result of war injuries in the First World War.

Although an NSDAP affiliated charity, it maintained a degree of independence in assets and organizational issues.
Together with the National Peoples Welfare (NSV) it was a charitable organization and supported health programs from its establishment till 1945.

By Law No. 5 (The Dinazification Decree) of the American Military Government dated 31 May 1945, the NAZI Party with all its institutions and organizations were disbanded.

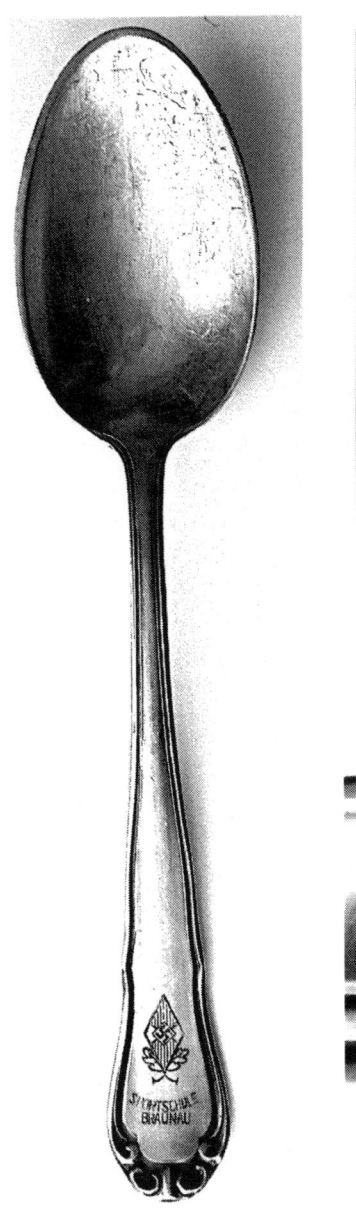

AD-83
212 mm / 8 6/16"

AD-83 HJ Sportschule Braunau

Soupspoon: Obverse carries the HJ emblem over 'Sportschule, Braunau. Reverse has unknown maker mark of 'EMD' with 90.

The HJ put more emphasis on physical and military training than on academic study.

In 1935, about 60 percent of Germany's young people belonged to the HJ. With the annexation of both Austria and Czechoslovakia in March of 1938, the various German created youth organizations (HJ, DJV, BDM & DJM) added over 1 million to their numbers and by 1939, about 82 percent (7.3 million) of eligible youths within the Greater Reich belonged making it the largest youth organization in the world. 1939 was declared "The Year of Physical Training" and introduced the Sports Competition. Medals were awarded to youths who performed rigorous athletic drills and met strict physical fitness standards. Every summer, a day would now be set aside as the "Day of the State Youth" for these events. School schedules were adjusted to allow for at least one hour of physical training in the morning and one hour each evening. Prior to this, only two hours per week had been set aside. Hitler also encouraged young boys to take up boxing to heighten their aggressiveness.

Note: this training center (Sportschule / Physical Training Academy) for selected HJ athletes was located in the town of Hitler's birth, Braunau, Austria after the 13 March 1938 annexation..

208

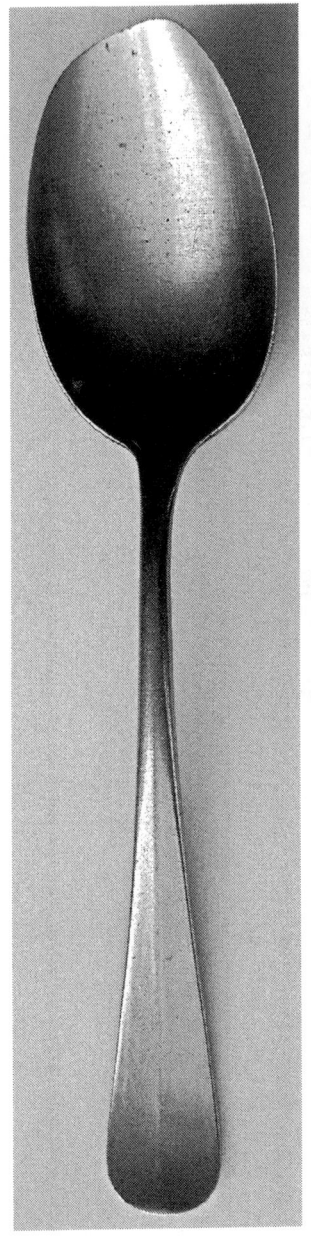

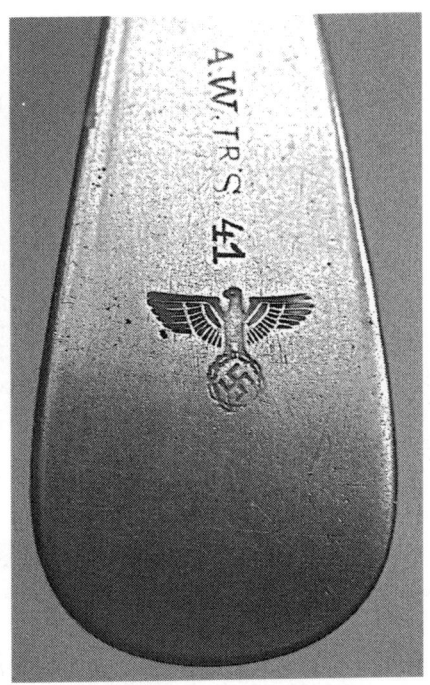

A.W.TR.S
41

ROSTFREI

AD-84
202 mm / 8"

AD-84 Heer

Tablespoon: Obverse unmarked with raised spine, reverse carries A.W.JRS 41

War in the East!

Germany invaded Poland 1 Sep 1939 with 53 divisions (6 armored and 4 motorized). The Western Front had 33 divisions behind the Siegfried Line (West Wall) short of manpower, heavy equipment, artillery and not fully trained. Only 11 divisions were considered fully efficient. France had some 70 divisions facing the Germans. Hitler was surprised when England and France declared war but was confident they would do nothing. In the event, France killed some 200 german soldiers and retired to the Maginot Line. England's philosophy was they could starve Germany into submission by sea control as they had done in WWI.

Germany's surprise attack on The Soviet Union started on 22 June 1941 with 3.2 M soldiers, 2,000 aircraft, 3,350 tanks, 7,184 pieces of artillery and 750,000 horses and in 10 days advanced 350 miles, started the Leningrad siege on 8 Sept 41 took Minsk in August and Kiev in Sept, reached Moscow suburbs in December. By the end of 1941, almost 1M Soviet jews had been murdered, all before the Wannsee Conference of Jan 42. The German approach has been cast as prepared to play tennis but the game was football as the depth of the front exceeded 1000 miles with a length of 2,500 miles! Something even German organization could not overcome.

note: It is 2,700 Km (1,675 miles) from Berlin to Stalingrad.

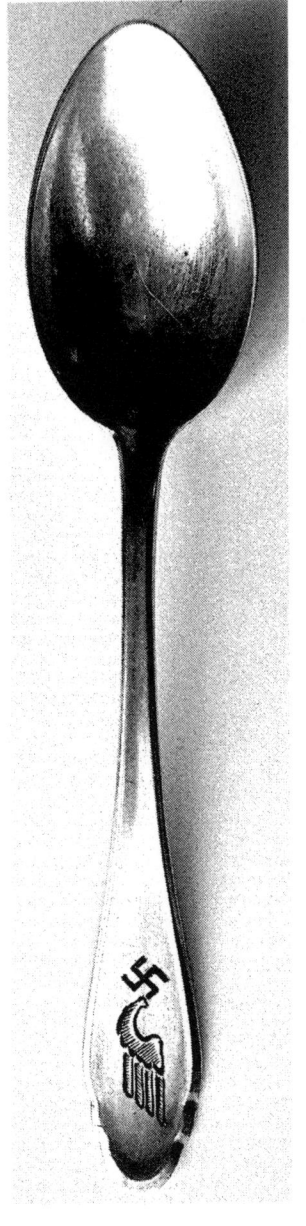

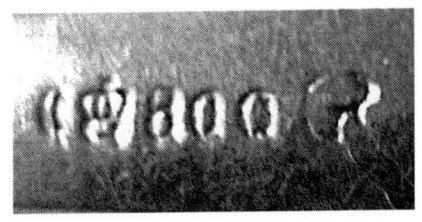

AD-85
141 mm / 5 9/15"

AD-85 Deutsche Reichsbahn (DR)

Teaspoon: On the obverse is the modified DR emblem where the original wheel has been replaced by a mobile swastika which became mandatory in 1937, Reverse carries crescent, crown, 800 and maker's mark GR (Gebruder Reiner, Krumbach Bayern 1910 - present).

During World War II, the Reichsbahn was an essential component of German military logistics, providing essential transportation services for the Reich throughout the occupied lands of Europe. In the East:

By 1 Sep 1939 - The DR had moved 86 non motorized divisions to the Polish border. During the Polish campaign, both sides participated in the destruction of the Polish rail system. The program to double the existing capacity for the invasion of Russia started In Oct 1940. By June 1941, east traffic was raised from 84 to 220 trains a day. 141 German divisions were moved to the Soviet border without detection.

From the Invasion of Russia on 22 June 1941 to 1 Jan 1943, the DR converted 22,000 miles of Soviet, wide gauge, rail to German standard gauge.

The DR's participation was crucial to the implementation of the "Final Solution of the Jewish Question". The Reichsbahn was paid to transport victims of the Holocaust from towns and cities throughout Europe to the Nazi concentration camp system and were paid by the track kilometer, so many pfennigs per Km. The rate was the same throughout the war. With children under ten going at half-fare and children under four going free. Payment had to be made for only one way. The guards of course had to have return fare paid for them because they were going back to their place of origin..."[1]

212

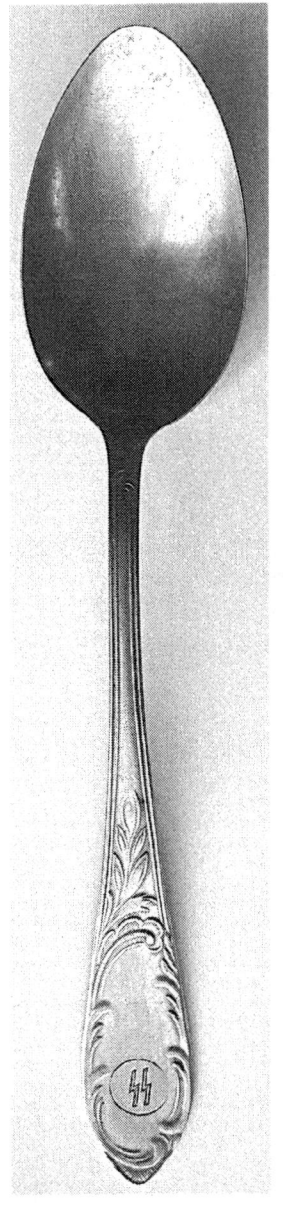

AD-86
211 mm / 8 5/16"

AD-86 SS

Tablespoon: Obverse carries the SS Runes in a circle while the reverse is maker marked 'neusilber'.

SS Regalia: Adopted as a link to the past, the Totenkopf (Death's Head) was the only common badge on all SS formations such as the Allgemeine-SS and Waffen-SS,

> From a 15th Century poem by Garnier von Susteren :
> Behold the Knight
> in solemn black manner.
> With a skull on his crest
> and blood on his banner

> The Stosstrupp Adolf Hitler adopted the Totenkopf in 1923 whose regimental song included:
> In black we are dressed,
> In blood we are drenched,
> Death's Head on our helmets.
> Hurrah! Hurrach!
> We stand unshaken!

The SS Runes was designed by Walter Heck in 1931 by combining two Sig-Runes side by side. The Sig-Rune was a symbol of victory.

SS motto: "To accept death and to hand out death"

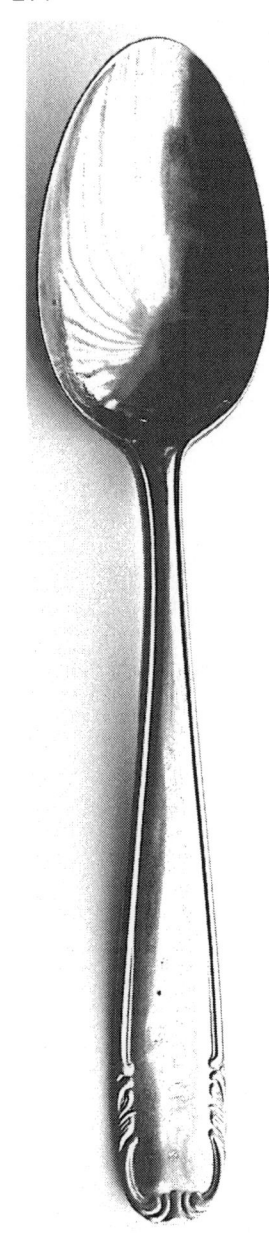

214

DAW
K.L.BUCHENWALD

ROSTFREI-INOX

AD-87
139 mm / 5 7/16"

AD-87 K.L.Buchenwald

Teaspoon, obverse clear, reverse carries DAW over K.L.BUCHENWALD, Rostfrei-Inox for Buchenwald Concentration Camp (Konzentrationslager Buchenwald)

The KLs were founded to isolate people viewed as "subversive dangers to the German race" and operated by the SS, completely outside normal German law. Buchenwald was established on Ettersberghill near Weimar, in 1937 and eventually grew to include 140 satellite camps or sub camps. The main gate's wrought iron inscription read, "Jedem das Seine" or "to Each his Own". As KL Buchenwald was on property of the German Reich, the SS actually purchased the camp's plants in the autumn of 1940 and founded a branch of the SS arms factory, Deutsche Ausrustungs Werke GmbH (DAW) employing from 500 to 1,400 inmates manufacturing wood and light metal products. The KL system was transferred to the SS Economic Administration Main Office in March 1942 due to a decision to engage concentration camp labor to support the war effort oriented primarily towards the wartime requirements of the Waffen-SS. Although not an extermination camp, the estimated camp death rate was 18% (43,000 of the 238,380 passing through from 1937 to 1945, with an additional 13,500 sent on to extermination camps bringing the total to 24%) Prisoners were marked with triangular camp badges of 7 colors: Red = political, Green = Police preventive detention, Black = 'work shy', Purple = Bible / religious, Blue = Emigrant, Pink = Homosexual and Yellow = Race Defiler. On 26Jan38, Himmler had issued an open arrest order for all able-bodied men "who have ascertainably refused 2 offers of employment without justification or have begun employment but quit it again after a brief time for no valid reason." - these were the "Work Shy"!

216

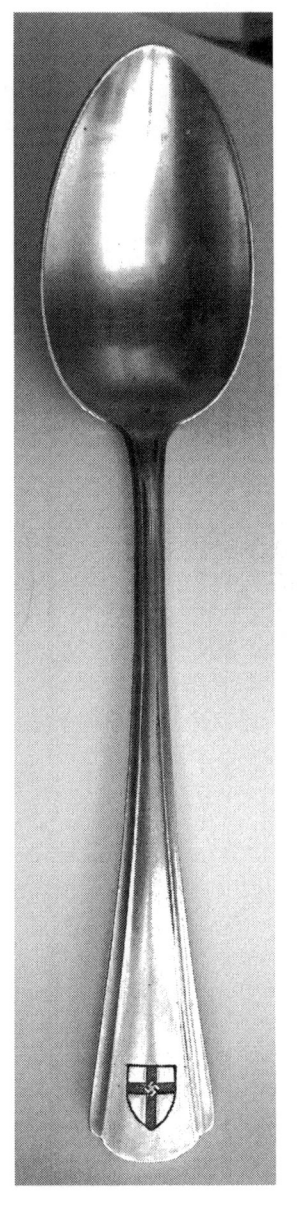

AD-88
218 mm / 8 9/16"

AD-88 Deutsche Christen - DC
(German Christians)

Tablespoon: The obverse carries the Deutsche Christen symbol of a Christian cross with a mobile swastika in the middle encompassed by a shield. Reverse maker marked Koch & Bergfeld of Bremen, (founded 1829), 800, crescent, crown. From Bishop Ludwig Mueller's service.

In 1932 the Protestant church came under the influence of the Nazi movement called "German Christians", (also called "Stormtroopers of Jesus"). The Deutsche Christen (DC) became the voice of Nazi ideology within the Evangelical Church and approved by Hitler, they proposed a church "Aryan paragraph" to prevent "non-Aryans" from becoming ministers or religious teachers. Only a very few Christians opposed Nazism such as the "Confessing Christians". The German Christian Movement was strongly nationalistic and adopted Luther's anti Semitism (ref his 1543 book, "On Jews and Their Lies") as well as his respect for authority (see Romans 13). Composed of the radical wing of German Lutheranism and the main Protestant branch supported the Nazi ideology, reconciling Christian doctrine with German nationalism and anti semitism. This movement represented Hitler's "Positive Christianity" views as lawfully encoded into the Nazi "constitution."

In the 1933 church elections, Hitler made a radio appeal in support of the German Christian movement and later appointed Ludwig Mueller, Reich Bishop of the Protestant Church. Bishop Mueller committed suicide in 1946!

Fact: In 1925, of the German population of 65 million, some 40 million were Evangelical Lutherans and 21 million Roman Catholics.

Some things that are to interesting to leave out

Army:Regulation H.Dv.300/1, TROOP COMMAND, a pocket sized, (4 1/4" X 6") gray paperbound booklet of 319 pages affectionately called "Aunt Frieda" (Tante Frieda, from its abbreviated title T.F. for Truppenfuhrung) postulated the basic principles of march, attack, pursuit, defense and other military operations for German commanders. The 1936, Berlin edition was in Fraktur typeface!, see OG-19.

Tanks: Total German Production: I's = 1,500, II's = 2,000, III's 5,644 (with 5,000 destroyed), IV's = 7350 (main battle tank), V's = 6,000 and VI's = 487 for a total of 22,981!

Tanks in service on 1 September 1939: I's = 1,445, II's = 1,226, I Command Tanks = 215, III's = 98 and IV's = 211. Of the 3,195 tanks, 1,251 were outside the armored divisions. During September 1939 only 57 tanks were produced and only 45 IV's were produced in all of 1939.

The Tiger I's fuel capacity was 534 liters (141 gals) which was estimated to take it 100 Km (62 miles) on road travel at 20 Km per hour and 50 Km (31 miles) cross country.

The PzKw VI, the Tiger II King Tiger / Konigstiger: Reportedly, 487 were produced. Used by the Schwere Panzer Abteiling of the Wehrmacht and the Waffen-SS on the Russian Front, Normandy, Holland Ardennes and the Battle of the Bulge. Powered by a 12 cylinder Maybach diesel, producing 700 hp, it ate 2 gallons of fuel per mile. The Henshel turret stored 86 rounds for the 88 mm main gun. With its massive 180 mm (7 inches) of frontal armor, the Tiger was virtually impervious to any allied fire. According to historical accounts, the front armor on the Tiger II was never breached in battle.

The 1942 Panzer Division was composed of four battalions each with 80 tanks. By mid-1943 the tank quantity was reduced to two battalions each with 50 tanks and a third battalion of tank destroyers.

At the Battle of Kursk (5-22 July 1943) the German's 700,000 men with 2,700 tanks fought the 1,000,000 Russians with 3,600 tanks. In the following 50 days, Germany lost 500,000 men and 7 panzer division (1,500 tanks)

Note: The US produced some 49,000 M4 Sherman tanks, initially with 2" of front armor and a 75 mm gun. The M4's gun could penetrate 2" of armor while German tanks could penetrate 4" to 6" of armor. The M4 was nicknamed 'Ronson' as it 'lights first time, every time" due to its gasoline fuel!
Russia produced 53,000 T-34 tanks with a 1944 run rate of 2,000 a month.

Halftracks (Spahpanzerwagon): a 7 ton vehicle able to run at 31 MPH, carried heavy machine guns and powered by a 6 cylinder Maybach engine. Some 14,000 were built

Krauss-Maffei Sd Kfz0; 11.5 ton prime mover with a 6 cylinder Maybach HL 62TUK, water cooled engine with 140 hp moving this 22 1/2' long behemoth at 50 km/h (31 mph). 12,000+ built. Associated with the towed 88 mm FLAK gun (Flug Aberhr Kanone)

Third Reich Special Days:

1 January   Day of National Awakening
20 April   Hitler's Birthday
1 May   National Holiday of the German People
9 Nov   Day of the Fallen of the Movement

The "Blood Flag" (Blutfahne) was shown three times a year: Party Anniversary, Annual Party Rally and the 9 November 1923 Commemorative march.

Submachine Guns:
Pistol caliber submachine guns reached their zenith during WWII. The Soviet PPSh41 (PE-PE-SHA) was the dominant submachine gun with 5.5 million manufactured, the British produced 4 million Stens, the US made 1.4 million Thompsons and Germany produced 910,000 MP-40's. Within a few years, they were little more than a footnote in the arena of military small arms, having been replaced completely in concept by the intermediate size cartridge assault rifle (Sturmgewehr) introduced by Germany in the late years of the war.

Cigarets: Although they were forbidden in the Luftwaffe and Allgemeine-SS, the US military sent as many as 425 million cigarets overseas monthly.

German Army (Heer) clothing seasons: The Winter season was from 15 September to 15 April.

Germany had 3 million deaths up till the last 9 months of the war, then 5 million more in the last 9 months for a total of 8 million.

The last Act: Did Hitler & Eva along with Goebbels & Magda end their lives in the Tristan and Isolde search for the realm of oneness, truth and reality, only to be achieved fully upon the deaths of the lovers? or did Hitler deliberately chose 30 April 1945 according to J.H. Brennam's observation, "The Dark Initiate had remained true to his black creed to the very last, had arranged his affairs so that even his suicide should be a sacrificial tribute to the Powers of Darkness. April 30 is the ancient Feast of Beltane, the day which blends into Walpurgis Night, It is perhaps the most important date in the whole calendar of Satanism."

Comments and corrections

As a result of the books lengthly production cycle, it allowed me to make the addition of (pages 199 - 221.

Ref Page 169 - Officers Field Besteck: German field officers have traditionally shared the enlisted men's food and eaten with the troops. There are many photos of Hitler, in the field with the troops and eating with them whereas the British and US have traditionally separated officers from the enlisted men with officers eating their own subsidized, superior rations in private.

Ref Page 173 - M-77: Per Wellner, the maker marks during the early VEB period used the earlier markings out of convenience. Another example of East German expediency or "why re-invent the wheel" was the continued use of the Heer's 'rain drop' pattern poncho used in 1944/45 and manufactured in the East for the 'Peoples Army' into the 50's.

Dated cutlery tends to disappear by 1943 when "Advancing on All Fronts" was a bitter memory and Germany suffered some 1,686,000 casualties that year.

Special Note

The German War Graves commission founded in 1919 maintains some 800 graveyards in 43 countries for 1.9 million German military 'victims of war'. Some 1.5 million WWII German military dead have not been 'clarified'. Search is now focused in the EAST for the 250,000 German MIA's in the Stalingrad area as well as Kursk, Smolensk, the Ukraine, Poland, Estonia-Latvia-Lithuania, the Slovakian Republic etc.

Donations are not US tax deductible but can be sent to:

>Volksbund Deutsche
>Kriegsgraberfursorge e.V.
>Bundesgeschaftsstelle
>Werner-Hilpert-Str.2
>34112 Kassel
>Deutschland

This organization publishes illustrated brochures locating all German military cemeteries and assists in the specific location of the fallen for family members. The edition covering Germany is some 100 pages. A second edition covers France, Belgium, Luxembourg and the Netherlands. The cemeteries are located on detailed maps with specific directions, comments and number buried by WWI or WWII. Due to funding constraints, all documentation is in German only.

FINI

First of all, thanks for buying this book and especially for actually getting to the end.

As you may know, this is my third, and last, book. The other two were:

> Astonishing Investment Facts and Wisdom
>
> and
>
> Astonishing Conservative Thoughts, Facts and Humor

And it is time to thank my beloved wife Gerda for her wonderful assistance with this book and her saintly patience with the first two.

Notes

Printed in Great Britain
by Amazon